EATING DISORDERS

EATING DISORDERS

DIANE YANCEY

Twenty-First Century
Medical Library

Twenty-First Century Books
Brookfield, Connecticut

To Monica, with deep appreciation.
Your commitment to help heal the minds of
troubled young people goes far beyond
professional responsibility.

Photographs courtesy of The Image Works: pp. 10 (© B. Daemmrich), 19 (© Esbin/Anderson), 45 (© Dion Ogust), 76 (© R. Lord); Sygma: pp. 14 (© Steve Schapiro), 59 (© Gregory Pace); Peter Arnold, Inc.: p. 22 (© Leonard Lessin); Monkmeyer: p. 39 (© Arlene Collins); Paul and Sandy Henrich: p. 63; Impact Visuals: p. 87 (© Brian Plonka); Photo Edit: pp. 97 (© Michael Newman), 123 (© David Young-Wolff); AP/Wide World Photos: p. 110

Library of Congress Cataloging-in-Publication Data
Yancey, Diane.
Eating disorders / Diane Yancey.
p.   cm. — (Twenty-first century medical library)
Includes bibliographical references and index.
Summary: Describes eating disorders such as anorexia, bulimia, and compulsive eating and discusses the causes, warning signs, diagnosis, and treatment.
ISBN 0-7613-0950-0 (lib. bdg.)
1. Eating disorders—Juvenile literature. 2. Anorexia nervosa—Juvenile literature. 3. Bulimia—Juvenile literature. 4. Body image—Juvenile literature.
[1. Eating disorders. 2. Anorexia nervosa. 3. Bulimia nervosa. 4. Body image.]
I. Title. II. Series.
RC552.E18Y36 1999 616.85'26—dc21 98-54834 CIP AC

Published by Twenty-First Century Books
A Division of The Millbrook Press, Inc.
2 Old New Milford Road, Brookfield, Connecticut 06804
www.millbrookpress.com

CONTENTS

Introduction
SIDETRACKED LIVES
9

Chapter One
WHAT ARE EATING DISORDERS?
16

Chapter Two
WARNING SIGNS AND SYMPTOMS
32

Chapter Three
ROOTS AND TRIGGERS
49

Chapter Four
RELATIVES AND RELATIONSHIPS
66

Chapter Five
GETTING HELP
82

Chapter Six
THE CHALLENGE OF RECOVERY
106

Chapter Seven
SUCCESS STORIES
120

GLOSSARY
130

RESOURCES
134

FURTHER READING
138

INDEX
140

EATING DISORDERS

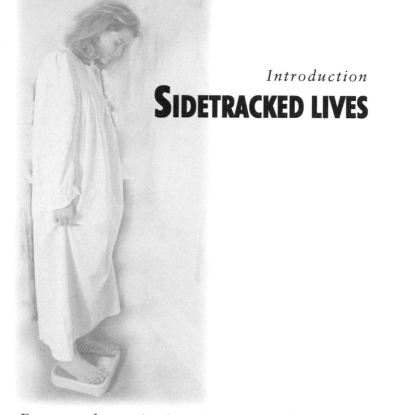

SIDETRACKED LIVES

For most of us, eating is an important and enjoyable part of life. We take pleasure in eating out at our favorite restaurants, feasting on turkey and pumpkin pie at Thanksgiving, and celebrating with ice cream and cake on our birthdays. Apart from special events, eating is often one of the high points of our day. Even something as simple as a peanut butter and jelly sandwich and a glass of cold milk can be the ultimate satisfaction when we are hungry.

For some teenagers, however, food becomes too important. Every waking moment is filled with thoughts and actions that revolve around eating, body size, and appearance. Many teens give up dreams and plans for the future, allow relationships with family and friends to deteriorate, and permanently impair their health, all because of mental conflicts, which they express through an obsession with food.

Many teens eat what could be considered "junk food," but even this can be part of a healthy person's normal eating habits. It's when food, weight, and appearance become an obsession that eating disorders are a threat.

In this book, you will read about several young people who are all too familiar with such harmful behavior. They have or have had eating disorders, crippling emotional and psychological disturbances, which are expressed as bizarre, unhealthy eating patterns. The teens featured in this book are representatives of real adolescents who prefer to remain anonymous. The quotes throughout may not be their exact words, but they do embody the innermost thoughts and feelings of the sufferers. All those who contributed to this book hope that their experiences will

aid and inform others who want to know more about—
or need help in overcoming—eating disorders.

Lori, 15 years old

Lori was a fine athlete, but she had always been a large
girl and hated her nickname, "the giant." At the age of
fifteen she was 5 feet 8 (173 centimeters), and weighed
185 pounds (84 kilograms). Her unhappiness with her
large size caused her to experiment with self-induced
vomiting. The experiment backfired, however. Lori
started devouring large amounts of junk food. Then, every time she ate something that she felt would make her
fat, she would run to the bathroom to throw up.

Ray, 18 years old

Ray developed an eating disorder after becoming involved
in bodybuilding when he was fifteen. Although he ate
large amounts of healthy food, he counted calories, measured everything he ate, and used his strict personal regimen to avoid facing any problems that arose in his life.
When a knee injury forced him to give up weight lifting,
he smothered his depression, emptiness, and loss with
large amounts of food. After he tipped the scales at 325
pounds (147 kilograms), Ray admitted to himself that
he had become a compulsive overeater who was severely
overweight.

Hannah, 14 years old

Hannah was a slender, attractive, fourteen-year-old who
believed she was never good enough in academics, sports,
making friends, and being a model daughter at home.
She worried that she was overweight, hated the fact that
she loved food, and became convinced that her life would
be better if she were thinner. When her 10-pound (4.5-
kilogram) weight loss went unnoticed by her schoolmates,
she continued to diet, increasingly afraid that she would

get fat if she stopped. Hunger made her irritable and anxious; almost everyone and everything made her angry.

Despite getting straight A's in school, Hannah was convinced that she was on the brink of failure and studied compulsively. Friendships and social events took second place to rigid eating constraints, strict study schedules, and periods of overwhelming depression and panic. Life became a black hole. No matter what she did, she could not be smart enough, thin enough, or perfect enough.

Michael, 18 years old

Michael had a traditional family background—his father was a police officer, his mother a stay-at-home wife who overprotected her son—and he found life at an eastern college a frightening and confusing experience. Extremely homesick, he quit eating, lost weight, and endured teasing by dorm mates about having AIDS. By the end of the first semester Michael had developed anorexia and was depressed enough to drop out of school and move back home. There, he focused full-time on his eating disorder— he was now bingeing and purging—and grew increasingly angry at his parents, who were always "on his back."

Kathy, 13 years old

Kathy came from an achievement-oriented family. Her parents were quiet, controlled, and discouraged their children from giving in to their feelings and emotions. Kathy was different—unsure, sensitive, emotional—and by the time she was fourteen, she was expressing her frustration and confusion through bingeing and purging. Her parents tried to control the problem by nagging, locking up food, and constantly supervising her bathroom visits, but that only served to escalate the problem. Finally, they turned to their family minister for advice. He recognized the power struggle that was tearing the family apart and wisely referred them to a professional counselor for therapy.

Liz, 16 years old

Liz was already deep in the throes of anorexia by the time her mother took her to their family physician for a checkup when she was sixteen. Two years before, both parents had supported her desire to lose 20 pounds (9 kilograms) and even allowed her to go through several weight-loss programs. Now she was extremely thin, and they were worried. When consulted, a poorly informed family physician didn't ask Liz about her eating habits. Instead, he urged caution, saying that Liz was "model thin." She returned home, where she continued to diet, binge, and purge.

By the time Liz was 20 pounds thinner, her anorexia was obvious, and her parents forced her to enter an inpatient clinic. In the following weeks, Liz was in and out of treatment. Depressed, angry, and full of self-hatred, she increased the frequency of her bingeing and purging rather than cooperate with professionals who tried to make her eat. Finally her body rebelled, and she suffered a heart attack. Only the quick response of her mother and paramedics saved her life.

Marcella, 28 years old

At 5 feet 5 (165 centimeters) and 275 pounds (125 kilograms), Marcella had been a compulsive overeater from her early teens. She had a problem with weight, came from a family of dieters, and had tried every diet in the book. Becoming a nurse hadn't helped. She was so busy taking care of others that food was her only luxury.

Marcella gained a lot of weight while caring for her brother during his painful and lingering illness and death, but this time eating wasn't enough to soothe her fatigue and depression. A case of post-traumatic stress disorder

The Carpenters were a popular brother-sister singing duo in the 1970s. Karen Carpenter's death in 1983 from an eating disorder helped bring national attention to the problem.

motivated her to seek help, and in counseling she began to explore the unexamined issues that had driven her to eat compulsively for years.

Eating disorders have been studied seriously only since the 1970s, when they began to affect significant numbers of teenagers in the United States, and did not gain public awareness until the death of singer Karen Carpenter on February 4, 1983. Thus, not even experts fully understand these complex disturbances. They disagree whether the causes and triggers are primarily physical or emotional. They are perplexed when the profiles of those who fall ill change over time. They differ concerning the most effective treatments and feel they must wait for a period of time before they know if disordered individuals can achieve long-term recovery.

For all the complexity of eating disorders, however, one fact is clear. These debilitating illnesses are more than simple problems with appetite and weight. Those who suffer from them do not lack willpower, as many people once believed, nor do they have weak, defective characters. As Nancy J. Kolodny points out in her book *When Food's a Foe*: "An eating disorder is a red flag, telling you that you need to pay attention to some situation in your life that you're ignoring or avoiding."

As you read on, you will see how complicated such disorders are, discover what makes certain teens vulnerable, and find out what treatments are available. As one expert states, "Eating disorders deserve our attention since they are one of the top ten problems facing American youth today."

Chapter One

WHAT ARE EATING DISORDERS?

Lori's Story

Lori had hated her body for as long as she could remember. She had been a big baby—more than 10 pounds (4.5 kilograms) and 24 inches (61 centimeters) long at birth—and remained taller and heavier than other girls her age. In high school she excelled at sports, but even that talent was not enough to boost her low self-esteem. "I was five foot eight and weighed one hundred eighty-five pounds. The kids called me 'the giant,'" she explains. "I ate healthy foods, but I was an 'extra large' when everyone else was 'medium.' Even my parents and sisters were slender. It just didn't seem fair."

When Lori was fifteen, one of her classes featured a presentation on eating disorders, and for the first time she learned how bulimics binge and purge. *"Making myself vomit was only an experiment at first, just to see if I could do it,"* she says. Subconsciously, however, Lori had discovered a way to express her poor self-esteem and her anger with her parents, particularly her father, who had a drinking problem and tried to control his family's lives.

What began as a casual experiment soon escalated into a habit that Lori saw as both shameful and disgusting. She would binge on junk food, then vomit it up to avoid gaining weight. Lori's parents discovered her purging one day and insisted that she visit an eating-disorder therapist who confirmed a diagnosis of bulimia nervosa. Lori attended counseling regularly, but anger kept her from really committing to anything her parents wanted her to do.

Lori's self-esteem sank lower after she graduated from high school and entered college. There, one of her coaches gave his team a lecture on the benefits of eating healthy. *"I felt so guilty—so bad about myself—thinking about all the junk I was stuffing in my face. So I went on another binge,"* she recalls. *"After that, it was like I couldn't control myself. The more I hated what I was doing, the more I did it."*

Then, one morning while Lori was purging, she vomited blood. *"I was so scared. I remember hearing about esophageal tears and knew this could be a sign of serious trouble. I didn't want to die, so I decided I'd better start getting well."* With her counselor's help, she began to explore the reasons for her disorder—poor self-esteem, perfectionism, and long-held resentments against her father. She also began the slow, difficult business of reducing the bingeing and purging that had gained such control over her life.

17

Ray's Story

Like Lori, Ray was a roly-poly baby. By the time he started school, however, he had become a skinny little boy, and his "nerdly" thinness in high school drew plenty of teasing from other boys. "When I complained to my folks, they basically told me to ignore it, get on with my life, everybody has problems of some kind," Ray says. Too angry to forget, but unwilling to fight back, Ray decided to lose his skinny image and began working out with weights in a neighborhood gym. To build up his muscles he also began taking steroids, hiding the fact from his parents.

By the time Ray was eighteen, he had biceps and pectorals to make any bodybuilder proud and was winning local bodybuilding competitions. He was also exercising obsessively, experiencing uncontrollable rages because of the steroids, and was totally preoccupied with food and body size. "I counted calories, measured each mouthful of food, and focused on my body just like a model or someone with an eating disorder," he says. "Any problems that came along, I just went to the gym and worked out for a few hours."

Then, while preparing for a competition, Ray slipped and dropped a weight on his knee. The damage was serious and required several surgeries. Ray's doctor also advised him to stop weight lifting for at least a year.

Ray obeyed, giving up the steroids as well, but soon sank into a deep depression. His life seemed empty without the only thing at which he had ever excelled. To complicate matters, he was still eating like a bodybuilder, and the extra calories were being stored on his body as fat. Frustrated and depressed, he began eating compul-

Physical activities that focus on appearance, such as bodybuilding, can trigger an eating disorder in at-risk teens. What begins as a healthful activity to achieve fitness can become an obsession.

sively, bingeing on all the junk food he had denied himself before. His weight skyrocketed to 325 pounds (147 kilograms).

To seek help for his depression, Ray went to see a counselor, who recognized that he had an eating disorder and began to treat him for that as well. Even though Ray had entered treatment voluntarily, his progress was slow. "The steroids had messed me up, and I had terrible eating habits. I'd never learned to listen to my body—to think about what foods made me feel good and which ones didn't. Then I had to deal with the feelings that had started the whole thing. That was the toughest part of all!"

UNDERSTANDING EATING DISORDERS

Countless teens like Lori and Ray suffer from eating disorders, the best known of which are anorexia nervosa, bulimia nervosa, and compulsive or binge eating. Many people perceive these illnesses as problems with the appetite or as a teen's desire to be thin and attractive. Although much about eating disorders is still a mystery, experts can say with certainty that anorexia, bulimia, and binge eating represent much more than that.

At least in part, eating disorders are subconscious ways by which some teens cope with poor self-esteem, anxiety, anger, and abuse. Those who develop them are focusing on weight and food because they have not learned more effective ways of solving problems and taking control of their lives. One therapist explains: "Defining anorexia and bulimia as a teen's simple desire to look good doesn't account for the self-destructiveness that accompanies the disorders and doesn't explain why teens continue their dysfunctional behavior until they are at death's door."

WHAT IS NORMAL EATING?

Before beginning a discussion on dysfunctional eating, it helps to define what "normal" eating is. Normal eating is a general term, since people have different eating patterns, food preferences, and nutritional needs. For instance, a 170-pound (77-kilogram) office worker might need 2,900 calories a day to function, while a 170-pound carpenter could burn 3,700 calories a day in support of his more energetic lifestyle. A teenage girl may fulfill her daily protein requirement by eating eggs, cheese, and soy products, while a teenage boy would do the same with hamburgers and pizza. The choices involved in normal eating are infinite.

To maintain good health throughout one's lifetime, however, most people need to follow certain nutritional guidelines when it comes to eating. But even if some people do not follow such guidelines closely, they are still considered normal eaters because they balance their nutritional needs over the course of several days. They also maintain certain behaviors and attitudes toward food. Authors Suzanne Abraham and Derek Llewellyn-Jones, in *Eating Disorders: The Facts*, describe normal eating as:

- eating something at least three times a day, with snacks between as guided by one's appetite;
- eating a wide variety of foods as part of a balanced and flexible diet;
- eating more of the food you enjoy when you wish to;
- eating more than you need to on some occasions;
- eating less than you need on some occasions;
- not eating for emotional reasons;

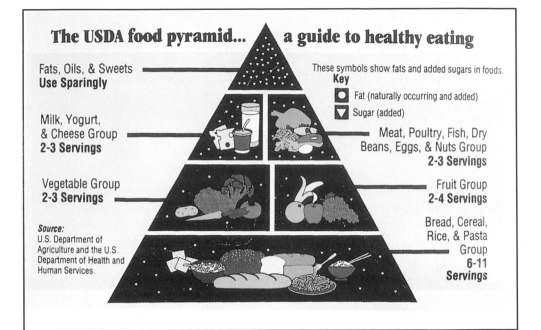

The USDA food pyramid... a guide to healthy eating

Fats, Oils, & Sweets
Use Sparingly

These symbols show fats and added sugars in foods.
Key
● Fat (naturally occurring and added)
▽ Sugar (added)

Milk, Yogurt,
& Cheese Group
2-3 Servings

Meat, Poultry, Fish, Dry
Beans, Eggs, & Nuts Group
2-3 Servings

Vegetable Group
2-3 Servings

Fruit Group
2-4 Servings

Source:
U.S. Department of
Agriculture and the U.S.
Department of Health and
Human Services.

Bread, Cereal,
Rice, & Pasta
Group
**6-11
Servings**

The Food Guide Pyramid is one way of grouping foods according to nutrient content. Health experts suggest that a person eat the recommended number of servings from each of its five food groups—bread and grains, vegetables, fruits, meats and beans, and milk products—daily.

- eating in a flexible way so that it does not interfere with your work, study, or social life, and vice versa;
- eating, when out socially, in a similar manner to the other people in the group;
- eating at fast-food outlets occasionally when you wish to or are with your friends;

22

- being aware that eating is not the most important thing in life but that it is important for good health and physical and mental well-being;
- being able to prepare food for yourself and others without feeling anxious;
- knowing what portions of food and size of meals are appropriate in different circumstances.

It is sometimes difficult to decide where normal eating ends and an eating disorder begins, since many teens have poor eating habits: They tend to skip meals, eat too much "junk food," and stuff themselves, for example, and are concerned with weight and appearance. Some studies find that 30 percent of otherwise healthy young women admit to having experienced one episode of disordered eating, and more than half of those admit to recurring episodes. Many young people eat for emotional reasons, or they eat too much and then starve themselves on a diet in order to lose weight.

Teens like these are at risk for developing eating disorders, but most can be considered healthy if friends, school, activities, and family are more of a priority than what thcy cat and how they look. The danger of an eating disorder begins when people and everyday activities take second place to dieting, or when a teen feels that food is the only thing that makes her happy.

EFFECTS OF EATING DISORDERS

The best-known eating disorder is anorexia nervosa, the ravaging effects of which have been highlighted repeatedly on television and in magazines. The term *anorexia*, which means "loss of appetite," is deceptive, since anorexics are often extremely hungry. Because of their distorted thinking, however, they gain enormous satisfaction from depriving themselves of food and are able to control their eating to such an extent that they can stunt their growth, suffer from malnutrition, and even starve themselves to death. Many anorexics go through periods of bingeing and purging as well, which puts additional stress on their bodies.

Bulimia nervosa, an eating disorder characterized by episodes of bingeing (eating large amounts of food in a short period of time) and purging (which includes vomiting, use of laxatives and diuretics, fasting and overexercising), is more common than anorexia. The disorder often begins with experimental, self-induced vomiting to get rid of unwanted calories, then quickly becomes a terrible compulsion. Bulimia is as harmful as anorexia, since those who suffer from it feel powerless to stop their self-destructive behavior. Lori's counselor points out: "Lori's decision to help herself when faced with life-threatening consequences showed great strength of character. Many bulimics continue to binge and purge even when confronted with serious illness and death."

Binge-eating disorder is similar to bulimia in that its victims experience uncontrollable urges to eat a large amount of food in a relatively short period of time. Those who suffer from it do not purge, however, and are usually significantly overweight. Compulsive overeaters are also overweight, but they may overeat all the time rather than binge. In both categories repeated, strenuous efforts to diet always fail.

Binge eaters and compulsive overeaters face all the risks associated with being overweight. Unlike those faced by anorexics and bulimics, however, such risks are usually long-term and do not prove threatening until later in life.

Since compulsive overeating is similar to binge eating, for ease of discussion the two categories will be combined in this book. The heading BINGE-EATING DISORDER will refer to both binge eating and compulsive overeating.

THE HISTORY OF EATING DISORDERS

The term *anorexia nervosa* was coined by an English physician, William Gull, in 1874, when he wrote of a young woman whose condition seemed to be one of simple starvation but who exhibited no physical cause for her emaciation. Gull noted that her symptoms included loss of appetite, constipation, slow pulse rate, and cessation of menstrual periods. He was struck by her restlessness and need for activity. "It seemed hardly possible that a body so wasted could undergo the exercise which seemed so agreeable," he wrote. Gull and other physicians and researchers identified anorexia as primarily a psychiatric (mental and emotional) illness, but research aiming at better understanding it produced confused results for many years. The work of eating-disorder pioneer Dr. Hilde Bruch from 1943 through 1984 contributed enormously to the knowledge of anorexia, but much more remains to be learned before the illness is fully understood.

Bingeing and purging were first described in ancient Roman times when citizens forced themselves to vomit in order to prolong their enjoyment of a heavy meal. In 1903, French psychiatrist Pierre Janet was one of the first to publish a description of a patient who binged and purged but never lost her appetite. American physician Albert Stunkard, an expert on obesity, identified bulimia in contemporary terms in 1959, but for many years the illness was considered a variation of anorexia. The American Psychiatric Association did not recognize bulimia as a distinct disorder until the 1980s and applied the term *bulimia nervosa* in 1987.

Until recently, binge eating was not considered a true eating disorder. Experts agreed, however, that people often overate for psychological reasons, and that symptoms exhibited by binge eaters were similar to some of those exhibited by anorexics and bulimics. Today, more and more eating-disorder therapists are treating clients for binge-eating disorder, even though formal diagnostic criteria do not yet exist. Since patients seeking treatment often find that their insurance will not cover the expense, many cannot afford treatment unless they also display symptoms of depression or some other well-defined psychiatric disorder.

WHAT CAUSES EATING DISORDERS?

No one can say definitely what causes eating disorders, although the organization Anorexia Nervosa and Related Eating Disorders (ANRED) lists eleven factors that seem to motivate teens to turn to such dysfunctional behavior. They are: to comfort themselves, to numb emotional pain, to avoid intimacy, to ask for attention, to escape from a demanding world, to express anger, to rebel against authority, to punish themselves, to release tension, to fill empty time, and to give themselves a sense that they are doing something important.

Not all teens deal with unhappiness and unsatisfied needs by eating dysfunctionally, however. There appear to be other factors, including personality traits and home environment, that are involved in the development of the disorders. Growing evidence suggests that there are physical and/or genetic roots as well, since teens with a family history of depression, addiction, or anxiety seem predisposed to developing eating disorders. Professionals also note that society is a likely influence, since it adds to teens' conflicts by sending contradictory messages—to remain thin while eating irresistible foods that are constantly advertised on television and in magazines.

This last factor might help explain why eating disorders have become more common since the 1970s. Eating-disorder specialists have long been puzzled by the increasing numbers, although many theories exist. Some experts see modern society, with its materialism and its ever-increasing preoccupation with success and achievement, as a possible catalyst. Some believe that society's emphasis on extreme thinness as an ideal for beauty is a motivating factor. Others point to the changing role of women, who face conflicting demands to be sexy, assertive, and career-oriented, while managing a home, being good wives and mothers, and molding their lives around the needs of others. They wonder if eating disorders are ways that young women retreat from the confusion involved in figuring out "who I ought to be."

WHO HAS EATING DISORDERS?

Females. Anorexia most often affects intelligent young women who are high achievers. It usually begins in the early to midteen years, although an increasing number of preteens have begun to exhibit symptoms. This age is a time when girls first come under strong peer pressure to be thin, to look good, and to fit in. It is also a time when the majority of girls, even the most attractive, have a shaky self-image. Bulimia strikes girls of high-school age, but it is most prevalent among young women in their late teens and early twenties, when the pressures of leaving home and becoming independent are greatest. Binge eating occurs among women of all ages but often develops in the teen years as well.

Eating disorders are almost unheard of in countries where life is a struggle for survival and food is scarce. In countries where everyone has plenty to eat, however, young women from middle- and upper-class families have traditionally been the most susceptible to the development of eating disorders. Recent evidence, however, shows that teens from lower-class families are exhibiting symptoms more than ever before.

Males. Young men make up only 5–10 percent of people with eating disorders since they are traditionally less concerned with thinness and appearance than young women. The number of males who are becoming anorexic, bulimic, and binge eaters seems to be growing, however. Part of the rise may be purely statistical—a greater willingness in young men to admit that they have a "girl thing," an eating disorder. Experts also point to increasing pressures on young men to succeed, be the best, and be competitive, as well as the trend among young men to think about physical appearance more than ever before. These experts argue that such factors may influence young men to eat dysfunctionally, just as similar pressures affect young women with a comparable outlook.

Participants in Low-Weight-Oriented Activities. Males and females involved in dance, athletics, and careers such as modeling are at great risk for developing anorexia, bulimia, or a combination of both. Such individuals place enormous emphasis on appearance, link leanness to successful performance and high achievement in their fields, and are often pressured to be thin by coaches and teachers as well. In one study, more than 60 percent of young female gymnasts admitted to regularly using unhealthy methods of weight loss such as vomiting, laxatives, diet pills, or fasting.

Minorities. In Western society, eating disorders occur primarily among Caucasian women, but no ethnic group is immune. Until recently, women of color seemed less prone to anorexia and bulimia, perhaps because thinness was not a prerequisite for beauty in their cultures or because many female role models on television have been of average size or even overweight. Studies now show, however, that blacks, Hispanics, and Asian-Americans are seeking help for such disorders with greater frequency. One reason for this could be that minorities are becoming familiar with the disorders and are getting treatment more often than in the past. Another reason may be that minorities are moving into higher social and economic brackets that place great emphasis on slenderness as a standard of beauty and as a stepping-stone to success.

HOW MANY PEOPLE HAVE EATING DISORDERS?

Since many people refuse to admit that they have an eating disorder, exact numbers are hard to obtain. Most experts estimate, however, that up to 10 percent of teenagers suffer from some type of eating disorder and that about 90 percent of them are female. The incidence of eating disorders is significantly lower among minority women than among Caucasian females.

Anorexia, the least common eating disorder, affects about 1 percent of teens in the United States. Bulimia, more common than anorexia, may affect up to 5 percent of adolescents overall, but the incidence among older teens is higher. For instance, one study of college students found that up to 20 percent of the female population suffered from bulimia.

Binge and compulsive eating are common to both males and females alike, but incidence is extremely difficult to determine. Studies indicate that more than one-half of adult Americans are overweight, and one-third are obese—that is, 20 percent or more above a normal, healthy weight. Not every large person is a binge eater or compulsive overeater, however. Experts can only estimate that the numbers of individuals suffering from binge-eating disorder range between 10 and 35 percent. As binge and compulsive eating are better understood as discrete eating disorders and are studied in greater depth, more accurate information will undoubtedly be available.

TREATMENT AND RECOVERY

Anorexia nervosa, bulimia nervosa, and binge-eating disorder are serious illnesses, which are seldom overcome without the help of a skilled therapist or counselor. Since studies show that eating disorders often have a biological basis, many patients benefit from antidepressants and other newly developed medications that help regulate the part of the brain involved in the disorder. "Taking a pill like Prozac won't cure an eating disorder," one specialist points out, "but it can ease the black depression that paralyzes many patients' thinking. You have to be able to function before you can begin the difficult process of recovery."

Even with the best of help, recovery is usually a long and difficult business. Disordered teens not only have to come to grips with unexplored emotional conflicts, but they also have to break their habit of using food as an outlet for their feelings. "I didn't realize it at the time, but I got obsessed with bodybuilding and fitness and diet to prove to myself and to all the guys who ignored me in school that I was better than they were," Ray says. "When I had to give that up, I was mad and scared. I didn't have anything else in my life. So I just kept eating, hoping the pain would go away."

Unlike recovered alcoholics and drug addicts, who can completely give up the substance they have abused, eating-disorder sufferers must face food every day and must constantly walk a fine line between too much and too little control. Before they can do that, however, they must recognize just how completely their disorder is affecting their lives. The signs and symptoms of eating disorders are explained in greater detail in the following chapter.

Chapter Two

WARNING SIGNS AND SYMPTOMS

Hannah's Story

Hannah was pretty, had boyfriends, came from a stable, supportive family, and made good grades. She suffered from bouts of depression but still had the motivation and talent to be successful in activities that ranged from playing the piano for the school choir to modeling for fashion shows at the mall. If Hannah agreed to help out with a project, she always did her best and finished the job to everyone's satisfaction.

Underneath Hannah's confident exterior, however, lay a negative mind-set that kept her from enjoying her accomplishments. Nothing that she—or anyone else—did was ever good enough, and as she grew older she became deeply depressed and desperately unhappy. Her good grades made her feel self-conscious and boring. She was me-

diocre in team sports and saw herself as awkward and uncoordinated. Shorter and rounder than the movie stars and models she idolized, she felt fat and hated the fact that she enjoyed food so much.

When she entered high school, Hannah decided she needed to control her appetite and went on a diet for the first time. She successfully shed 10 pounds (4.5 kilograms) and was proud of her loss, even though none of her friends seemed to notice. "I didn't let it show, but I was hurt. They paid attention to other, more expressive people—even commented on how skinny other girls were. It made me feel invisible."

Losing weight didn't agree with her physically—her stomach hurt and felt bloated—but Hannah continued to diet, afraid that if she ate normally she would get fat. When friends asked her out, she often refused, both because she didn't have fun and because she would have to eat. "I used homework as an excuse, too, and I studied all the time. To me, getting a B was failure. But I found it harder and harder to concentrate. I was having terrible headaches and stomachaches. Sometimes my heart would beat so fast I was afraid I was having a heart attack."

Aware that their daughter was losing weight, Hannah's parents took her to their family doctor who referred her to an eating-disorder clinic. Hannah resisted. "I was angry at them for trying to make me eat. I also remember thinking that I couldn't be anorexic because I hadn't lost enough weight yet." A therapist at the clinic disagreed. Hannah's distorted perception of her body, her perfectionism and need for control, her excessive exercise routines, and countless physical symptoms all indicated that she had anorexia nervosa.

Hannah's progress toward recovery was complicated by her reluctance to enter treatment, her depression, and her obsessive-compulsive impulses, which made it hard for her to change her way of thinking and her approach to life. "I felt hopeless, but also proud of my glamorous problem and jealous of girls who had gotten down to really low weights," she explains. "They were more successful."

Her negative outlook made her skeptical of everything her counselor suggested, and she resisted taking medication to ease her depression. "It took a lot of strength for me to finally decide to take antidepressants, because I like to do things myself. And I hated the side effects. It took me a few years to find the right stuff to take."

After several years of treatment, Hannah has taken steps toward recovery, although she gets frustrated with herself, other people, and life in general. "I thought I was going to feel better than this. I thought I was going to be happier and that life was going to be easier."

DIAGNOSTIC CRITERIA FOR EATING DISORDERS

When diagnosing eating disorders like Hannah's, health professionals refer to criteria listed in the fourth edition of the *Diagnostic and Statistical Manual of Mental Disorders* (DSM-IV), published by the American Psychiatric Association.

For a diagnosis of anorexia nervosa to be made, the following symptoms must be present:

- Refusal to maintain body weight over a minimal normal weight for age and height—for example, weight loss leading to maintenance of body weight 15 percent below that expected; or failure to make expected weight gain during period of growth, leading to body weight 15 percent below that expected.

- Intense fear of gaining weight or becoming fat, even though underweight.

- Disturbance in the way in which one's body weight, size, or shape is experienced—for example, the person claims to "feel fat" even when emaciated, believes that one area of the body is "too fat" even when obviously underweight.

- In females, absence of at least three consecutive menstrual cycles when otherwise expected to occur.

For bulimia nervosa, the following symptoms must be present:

- Recurrent episodes of binge eating; rapid consumption of a large amount of food in a discrete period of time.

- A feeling of lack of control over eating behavior during the eating binges.

- The person regularly engages in either self-induced vomiting, use of laxatives or diuretics, strict dieting or fasting, or vigorous exercise in order to prevent weight gain.

- A minimum average of two binge-eating episodes a week for at least three months.

- Persistent overconcern with body shape and weight.

At present, binge-eating disorder falls under the category "Atypical Eating Disorders Not Otherwise Specified" in the DSM-IV. The category also includes variations of anorexia and bulimia. Formal diagnostic criteria for binge-eating disorder have been proposed, however, and symptoms would include:

- Recurrent episodes of binge eating (rapid consumption of a large amount of food in a discrete period of time).
- A feeling of lack of control over eating behavior during the eating binges.
- Binge-eating episodes are associated with at least three of the following:

  eats more rapidly than usual

  eats until feels uncomfortably full

  eats large amounts of food when not feeling hungry

  eats alone; is embarrassed about how much is eaten

  feels disgusted with oneself; feels depressed or guilty about overeating.
- Binge eating occurs on the average at least two days a week for six months or more.
- Eating behavior does not occur exclusively during the course of anorexia nervosa or bulimia nervosa.

While only the above indicators need be present to diagnose anorexia, bulimia, and binge or compulsive eating, there are, in fact, numerous behavioral, physical, and psychological symptoms that are common to each. A more complete discussion of these symptoms follows.

ANOREXIA NERVOSA

Behavioral Symptoms

Restricted eating and a powerful fear of being fat are two of the most widely known behavioral symptoms of anorexia nervosa. These feelings usually have nothing to do with a teen being overweight. Many anorexics have never been fat. Because of a distorted body image, however, they see themselves as overweight, and their symptoms do not lessen as they lose weight. "My thighs stuck out further than my hips, and my waist was thick. The actress Julia Roberts was the American ideal at the time, and I didn't measure up," Hannah explains.

Anorexics avoid places and situations where they may have to eat, but since they constantly think about food, they often collect recipes and bake delectable goodies that they give away or encourage others to eat. When they do eat, they take small portions and "play" with their food—cutting it into small pieces, chewing each bite a given number of times, or rearranging it on their plates. "A dinner plate of food made Hannah panic," her mother remembers. "She would first take a tiny portion of meat or casserole, then, after her plate was empty, she'd take a few vegetables. Later she'd allow herself a spoonful of ice cream or some bread, but she usually ate it standing in front of the refrigerator."

Anorexics are proud of their rigid control but fear that others will try to force them to eat. Rather than show off their weight loss, they dress in loose, layered clothing that hides their emaciated state. Some anorexics, like Hannah, are able to restrict calories for years and are classed as having the restricting type of anorexia. For others, their gnawing hunger compels them to eat. Up to one-third turn to purging in order to maintain a low weight. This variation of anorexia, known as the binge-purge type, is distinguished from bulimia in that binge-purge anorexics maintain their weight at an extremely low level. Bulimics often maintain a relatively normal weight.

Physical Symptoms
The physical signs of anorexia nervosa may not be apparent to the casual observer, since anorexics are not al-

ways skeletally thin. Most, in fact, are comparable in size to other slender young women in today's society. Even after they have lost a great deal of weight, anorexics may be praised and rewarded for their weight loss by friends who are envious of their willpower or by boys who equate thinness with attractiveness. Some gravely ill anorexics have been approached by modeling representatives who promise them a successful career because they meet society's standards of thinness and beauty.

Weight loss is only one physical symptom of anorexia, however. Since most anorexics have little fat on their bodies, they feel cold, even in the warmest weather. They develop dry skin and soft, downy fuzz, called lanugo hair, on their arms and other parts of their bodies as their systems struggle to retain warmth in the absence of a necessary amount of fat. Because they are malnourished, their nails and hair may become brittle or quit growing altogether. Their stomachs hurt, they are constipated, and they complain of feeling bloated. Most are highly uncomfortable in their underweight bodies and avoid any kind of bodily contact. "I drove myself crazy finding jeans that wouldn't touch my waist," Hannah says. "But then they would hang on my hip bones, and that irritated me, too."

Anorexics suffer from dizziness, fainting spells, rapid heartbeat, and poor concentration. They are always tired but have trouble sleeping. Female anorexics experience amenorrhea, a cessation of menstrual periods resulting from low levels of fat in their bodies. Without medical treatment, malnutrition and low estrogen levels lead to osteoporosis (a degenerative bone disease), heart muscle damage, heart irregularities, and loss of brain mass. Death is the ultimate danger. The risk increases in proportion to the length of time a person has been anorexic, from a 5 percent mortality rate among those who have been ill for five years to as high as 20 percent among those who have suffered thirty years or more.

To burn off fat and calories, anorexics become hyperactive, always moving restlessly, sleeping only a few hours a night, and setting up a rigid and excessive exercise schedule.

Psychological Symptoms

Along with physical and behavioral changes, anorexics exhibit all the psychological symptoms of people who are starving. They are depressed, irritable, and pessimistic. Most anorexics are very bright young women who drive themselves to excel in school and careers, but they get no pleasure from their achievements. Hannah says, "I was never good enough; nothing ever satisfied me."

Anorexics' friendships suffer since they have no time or energy for anything except thoughts of food. They label anyone's efforts to get them to change their eating habits as jealousy or faultfinding. "When I went to a restaurant, waiters would comment on how little I ate," Hannah says. "I'd get embarrassed and angry, like who were they to criticize me?" As relationships suffer and anorexics become more isolated, they conclude that they are not "good enough" to have friends and withdraw further into a preoccupation with their disorder, which eventually occupies every waking hour and sometimes spills over into bizarre food-related dreams.

BULIMIA NERVOSA

Behavioral Symptoms

Bulimics can be perfectionists or underachievers, teens with active social lives or introverts who are withdrawn and alone. All are preoccupied with food and weight and fear becoming fat if they discontinue their behavior. The eating patterns of bulimics are less controlled than those of anorexics; some experts describe them as chaotic, since they are so extreme and unrestrained. Theirs is an all-or-nothing approach—once they start eating they can't stop until they are sick or run out of food. Unlike anorexics, bulimics turn to food rather than away from it in an effort to cope with their unexpressed emotional problems.

While bulimics often eat normally in public, in private they compulsively eat large amounts of food—usually high-calorie, easily-ingested food such as ice cream, cookies, chips, or doughnuts—in a very short time. Bulimics can consume thousands of calories at a sitting, eating until everything is gone or until they are too sick to continue. The taste of food becomes unimportant as they push it into their mouths and gulp it down almost without chewing. "When I binged, I didn't taste anything," Lori says. "It was 'shovel it in and swallow it down,' like a machine, over and over. My hands would shake. I'd breathe fast. Sometimes I'd be crying, it was so terrible."

Binges are followed by periods during which bulimics fast, exercise too much, practice self-induced vomiting, and/or take laxatives and diet pills. "I won't describe exactly how to purge, because that's how I learned, from somebody else," Lori explains. "It was easy, though." Bingeing and purging may occur only occasionally early in the disorder, but many teens soon find it hard to resist behavior that they first saw as "a onetime thing." Episodes can become as frequent as several times a day. Some teens seem proud of their behavior, perceiving it as a superior way to maintain their weight. Most realize that their eating patterns are abnormal, however, and often become more secretive as time passes and they become more involved in their disorder.

Physical Symptoms

Since bulimics are able to maintain a normal weight, their disorder is almost invisible unless someone catches them bingeing or purging or recognizes telltale signs like bad breath, bloodshot eyes, broken blood vessels under the eyes, or a finger callus that develops from repeated self-induced vomiting.

The disorder has serious, hidden physical consequences, however. Stomach acids erode tooth enamel and irritate the esophagus, throat, and mouth. The stress of vomiting can cause esophageal tears or ruptures, sore throat, and a characteristic swelling of overstimulated salivary glands (which may cause "chipmunk cheeks"). Over time, the stomach empties more slowly, resulting in a feeling of bloating. The use of diuretics (water pills) can lead to dehydration, while the prolonged abuse of laxatives can cause intestinal malfunction, even shutdown.

Repeated vomiting upsets the body's delicate chemical equilibrium. The continued loss of stomach acid brings on a physical condition called "alkalosis," with symptoms that include weakness, fatigue, pounding headaches, and feelings of anxiety. Loss of important minerals can also lead to muscle cramps, irregular heartbeat, and in the worst cases, cardiac arrest and death.

The death rate from bulimia appears to be lower than that from anorexia, although the disorder has not been studied long-term. Some reports suggest that the outlook for people with severe bulimia may be bleaker than that for individuals with the restricting type of anorexia.

Psychological Symptoms

Bulimics may appear happy, but inside they are depressed, ashamed, and self-critical. They know that they are out of control. Their moods swing dramatically between elation and sadness and are dependent on the bulimics' weight, how full they feel, and if they have recently binged or purged.

Bingeing and purging have a "numbing" effect on bulimics, since these are highly emotional acts and, once completed, leave them too tired to feel anything at all. Bingeing itself seldom occurs because of hunger: It is usually a reaction to boredom, anger, anxiety, or some other emotion. It can be either pleasurable or painful. For some bulimics, eating large amounts of food at top speed helps release tension. Once finished, however, they feel sick, consumed with self-hate, and restless until they have purged. For others, bingeing is only a necessary step to get through in order to have something to vomit. This vomiting is what eases pain and tension, leaving the bulimic feeling empty and lighter. Feelings of well-being are always temporary, however, and soon the bulimic feels a compulsion to begin the cycle again.

For those teens who are motivated by a subconscious desire to punish themselves, the more painful the binge-purge cycle is, the more their needs are satisfied. "Just before I collapsed, I went through a whole cycle once an hour for hours on end," says Liz, who suffers from the binge-purge form of anorexia. "I think part of me knew I was killing myself, but the part that was in control wouldn't let me stop." Bulimia is much like an addiction; in fact, experts have discovered that up to 30 percent of all bulimics abuse drugs or alcohol as well as food. Many bulimics claim it is as difficult to stop purging as it is to give up cigarettes or drugs.

BINGE-EATING DISORDER

Behavioral Symptoms

Unlike anorexia nervosa and bulimia nervosa, binge eating is not yet accepted by some professionals and insurance companies as a valid type of eating disorder. This is partly because, in our society, a variety of factors may contribute to overweight and obesity. Many people have poor eating habits, or eat too many high-fat, high-calorie foods, and get too little exercise. Some people seem to be genetically predisposed to be fat. Some appear to have greater numbers of fat cells in their body, which tend to store fat.

Experts agree, however, that for many people there is a psychological component to eating. Many binge eaters have a mental and emotional outlook similar to that of anorexics and bulimics, and their behavior around food is often much the same. Like other eating-disordered individuals, binge eaters are obsessed with food. "I thought about it, looked forward to it, and worried about it constantly," Ray says. "I linked everything that happened to food. I ate when I felt left out, when I felt worried, when something disappointing happened. When something good happened, I ate to celebrate. When *nothing* happened, I ate out of boredom."

Binge eaters usually take smaller-than-normal servings when they eat with others. Alone, however, they give in to their compulsion. Some go from restaurant to restaurant, eating meal after meal. Some retreat to the privacy of their homes, where they can eat continuously, devouring food that they do not even enjoy—cans of cold spaghetti or boxes of dry cake mix. Once started, many continue to binge until they are in pain or until something or someone interrupts them. Compulsive overeaters are less dramatic in their food habits, preferring to nibble and snack their way through the evening hours. "I kept myself busy during the day," says Marcella, explaining her compulsive-eating patterns. "But the evening, after the work was done, was my time. I didn't have to rush, and I had a whole kitchen full of food to choose from."

Since binge eaters and compulsive overeaters long to be thin, they are always in some stage of a diet—planning one, suffering through one, or breaking one. Most have tried every known diet, from low-calorie liquid protein drinks and packaged meal programs to plans that rely on bizarre food combinations and restrictions that promise to burn calories quicker. Many have also tried an endless variety of drugs, gimmicks, and techniques that include over-the-counter diet pills, prescription drugs

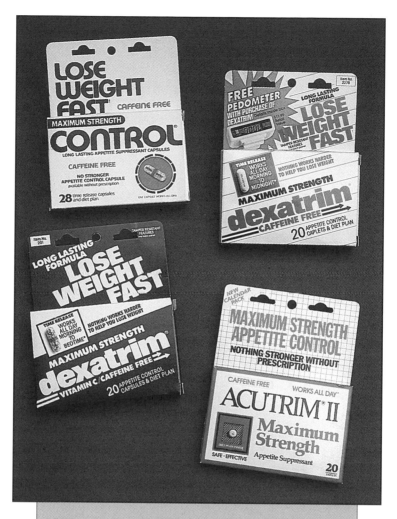

Binge and compulsive eaters, always engaged in a struggle to lose weight, sometimes turn to over-the-counter remedies that promise quick weight loss. But these usually fail to produce the desired results, as do other methods, since dieters haven't addressed the emotional reasons for their overeating.

such as dexphenfluramine (Redux) and fenfluramine-phentermine (fen-phen), body wraps, herbal teas, and aromatherapy. While some of the most drastic methods, such as jaw wiring and gastric bypass, do result in temporary weight loss, most techniques end in failure. Dieters, having done nothing to address their emotional reasons for eating, rebound from days or weeks of deprivation. They eat more than they did before and in no time at all regain the weight they lost and more besides.

Physical Symptoms

Binge and compulsive eaters are chronically overweight, often obese. They deal with daily physical problems such as shortness of breath, fatigue, and an inability to run or participate in sports as easily as persons with lower weight. When dieting strictly for a long period of time, binge eaters may experience many physical symptoms common to anorexia—fatigue, cold intolerance, hair loss, abdominal pain, and others.

The long-term implications of being overweight are more serious, however. Since binge eaters suffer from poor self-esteem and an obsession to be thin, the risk of developing anorexia or bulimia is high. Binge eaters are also at risk for diabetes, high blood pressure, heart attack, and stroke. They are more likely to develop gallbladder disease, various forms of cancer including breast cancer, and often suffer complications during surgery and during childbirth. Those who are significantly overweight often suffer from arthritis and problems with their joints that seriously affect mobility. Some are eventually confined to a wheelchair.

Psychological Symptoms

Binge eaters appear to be happy and content, but when they are alone they are sad, lonely, frustrated, and empty. They have poor self-esteem and try to win acceptance by putting the needs of others ahead of their own. Like Marcella, who became a nurse, some are caregivers and people-pleasers, neglecting their homework to bake a birthday cake for a friend or giving away a prized possession to someone who only casually admired it.

Binge eaters are always afraid that what they do will not be good enough, and so they are tense and self-critical. When their efforts fail to fill the emptiness inside, they turn to food for solace. As Marcella says, "I looked for companionship and comfort from food. When I was eating, I felt a sense of warmth and well-being."

Binge eaters are usually ashamed of their overweight bodies. The rejection and discrimination they encounter only adds to their self-disgust. "I was never openly insulted, but I was still sensitive," Marcella says. "When I walked down the aisle of a store and saw someone look at me and then glance away, I always thought it was because I was so heavy." Many binge eaters, therefore, mentally disconnect from their bodies and see themselves as thin people trapped in, or hiding behind, their fat. Most constantly fantasize about being thin, convinced that they will be happier, more popular, and more successful as soon as they lose weight.

SEVERITY OF SYMPTOMS

There are no formal criteria to specify "mild," "moderate," or "severe" levels of eating disorders, but disordered behavior does cover a range of severity.

Eating disorders are usually less intense in their early stages and grow progressively worse—with greater restriction of calories or more frequent bingeing and purging—as time passes, particularly if teens reject treatment. Those who exhibit all the symptoms of a disorder but binge only two times a week or have lost only 15 percent of their body weight would generally be perceived as having mild or moderate symptoms, although factors such as deep depression or suicidal thoughts would affect the assessment.

Teenagers are considered severely anorexic when they have lost a large percentage of their original body weight, are at a dangerously low weight, or have to be hospitalized because of a life-threatening complication resulting from their disorder. Bulimics are considered severely ill when they binge and purge frequently and repeatedly or when they have to be hospitalized for complications resulting from bulimia.

Even at their mildest, eating disorders are serious and should not be ignored or taken lightly. Once involved in disordered thinking, it is rare for a teen to give in to parental demands and "just stop" dieting or throwing up. And just because a physician judges a teen to be at low risk for serious complications, it does not mean that he or she is truly safe. "Liz had been to the doctor for tests just a few days before her heart attack," her mother explains. "There were no signs of what was coming. We were taken completely off guard."

Teens with eating disorders are desperately unhappy with themselves but often do not understand the reasons for their unhappiness or the roots of their dysfunctional eating. Factors that predispose a teen for an eating disorder, as well as triggers that set off dysfunctional eating, are explored in the following chapter.

Chapter Three

ROOTS AND TRIGGERS

Michael's Story

Michael's eating disorder began when he was eighteen, the year he left home for the first time. Always a small, sensitive boy, he had grown up in a family where his homemaker mother protected him from his police-officer father, who had a tendency to verbally abuse the family.

Having been sheltered all his life, Michael found that leaving home for a distant college in the East was harder than he had ever imagined. He had never been away from home before, just as he had never lived with people of different races, religions, and backgrounds. He felt out of place, said stupid things, and found it hard to make friends. His homesickness was deepened by a breakup with his girlfriend shortly before leaving home.

Lonely and unhappy, Michael's appetite suffered, and he began losing weight. This loss, coupled with his small size and poor social skills, left him open to hassling from his rowdy, rough-and-tumble dorm mates. "They began asking me if I had AIDS. Some of them started the rumor I was gay. It really shook me up," he remembers.

At the end of the first semester, Michael dropped out of school and returned home. There, depressed, angry, and full of self-hatred, he began bingeing and purging, practicing minor forms of self-mutilation such as cutting himself with razor blades, chewing his fingernails to the quick, picking endlessly at scabs, and experiencing uncontrollable rages. He blamed himself for his inadequacies. He blamed his parents for failing to prepare him for adulthood. He blamed college for being so difficult and unfair. His father's verbal tirades and his mother's disappointment only made things worse. Finally, after trying unsuccessfully to knock his father down during an argument, Michael agreed to get help at an inpatient eating-disorder clinic. "I did it to get my parents off my back," he says.

His first experience with therapy was brief and did Michael little good since he had only reluctantly agreed to go. Several months later, however, he went on his own to an outpatient clinic. "I was scared. I had this dream that I had died and was at my own funeral—a real old-fashioned Irish wake. When I woke up, I'd been asleep, or maybe unconscious, for twenty-three hours."

Despite his willingness to enter treatment, Michael found it difficult to change his behavior and his self-destructive ways of thinking. His old friends were away at college or making new lives for themselves. His poor self-esteem made him afraid to reach out to others or to try anything new. His poor health earned him much attention, particularly from his mother, on whom he had grown very dependent. In fact, as his counselor pointed out, Michael had no life other than his eating disorder.

THE ROOTS OF AN EATING DISORDER

While experts can recognize the symptoms of an eating disorder, they are unable to determine with certainty who will develop one and who will not. They have, however, identified certain predisposing factors involving personality traits, home environment, genetics, and social pressures, that, when combined, make teens particularly susceptible to eating disorders.

Dissatisfaction with Body Image

Many adolescents are unhappy with their body size and shape, but severe dissatisfaction is common to all teens who develop eating disorders. These young people are prone to look in the mirror, focus on their flaws rather than their attributes, then exaggerate those flaws and label themselves "fat," "stocky," or "ugly," when in fact they are none of those things. "I didn't listen when the counselor pointed out that I'd never been fat. She even had me bring in pictures of myself as a kid. It didn't matter. All I could see was my fat face," remembers Kathy.

Since looks are so important to teens with severe body image dissatisfaction, they often begin to judge their worth by appearance alone and may decide that they have to improve their image and themselves by dieting. Their distorted perception of themselves is not changed by weight loss, however, and because they are highly self-critical, they never achieve the perfect image they have created in their minds.

51

Poor Self-Esteem

Poor self-esteem is a quality shared by almost all eating-disordered teens. As one expert explains, "Self-esteem is the way you feel about yourself, the way you make decisions, act around friends, handle stress, etc. If you have poor self-esteem, it is likely you will see yourself as stupid, worthless, or inferior."

Poor self-esteem may be a response to hurtful family interactions, discouraging experiences in school, or unreasonable messages from society. Since teens with poor self-esteem feel inferior, they are seldom comfortable or content with themselves. Some feel so powerless and overwhelmed with life that they begin concentrating on their bodies as the one thing they can control. Many eating-disordered teens describe their poor self-image as a feeling of emptiness, which they unsuccessfully try to fill with food or with achieving the perfect body. "My eating problems were sort of a self-destructive hobby," Michael says. "They gave me a focus in life."

All eating-disordered teens crave the respect and admiration of others but are convinced that they are not good enough to deserve them. "I shy away from people I admire," Hannah says. "I don't even give them a chance to get to know me." Often, disordered teens go to astonishing lengths to be accepted—allowing themselves to be unfairly treated or blamed for something they have not done. They feel angry when this happens, but they stifle their anger, believing they do not deserve the right to express themselves.

Negative Mind-set

Eating-disordered teens not only suffer from feelings of inferiority and worthlessness, but they are convinced that society looks down on them. This negative mind-set seems to be an underlying condition—a way of looking at life—

that may be inherent in their personalities or may have developed in response to childhood experiences.

No matter what the cause, such teens are pessimists at heart, convinced that the worst is going to happen, braced for a putdown or a criticism. Even those who seem happy and outgoing are certain that everyone looks at them with disapproving eyes, ready to blame, ready to attack. Michael says, "I've always been afraid that people won't like me. Maybe it's because I have a hard time liking people. I'm very critical, and I guess I assume that they feel the same."

Perfectionism

Eating-disordered teens—anorexics in particular—are often perfectionists who demand the impossible from themselves in school, sports, appearance, and relationships. Many will avoid a new activity if they are not sure they can do it well. This perfectionism leads them to think in black-and-white terms. For instance, if they do not make A's in school, they will flunk out; if they cannot be the best member of the team, they will not play at all. Lori's counselor observes, "In her mind, Lori equated 'big' with 'fat,' and anyone who was fat was unhealthy. Then she had herself fat-tested and discovered that she was very lean. Her weight was largely muscle. It took several months for her to reconcile the facts—she was large but not fat."

Teens who are perfectionists easily forget their many successes, dwell on past mistakes, and hate themselves for their failures. Most are consumed with worry when they think of the future and all its uncertainties. Hannah's mother says, "In high school Hannah would push herself for perfect scores on each test and assignment because she might fail the next one and ruin her chances to get into college. Even when she graduated with high hon-

53

ors, she couldn't relax, because she was afraid she would fail at college and ruin her chances to get a good job."

Suppression of Feelings

Teens with eating disorders are poor at expressing their feelings even to themselves. This may be because they are naturally quiet people who do not easily put their thoughts into words. It may be that they come from families where communication is not encouraged, or because they are convinced that what they think and say will be considered "stupid."

Many eating-disordered teens are ambivalent in their feelings—they experience opposite or conflicting emotions at the same time and don't know how to handle such feelings. They hate their bodies but are obsessed with them. They want their parents' approval but feel rebellious and angry. They want to be independent but are afraid of being on their own.

For whatever reason, eating or not eating becomes a way of coping with or expressing these conflicting feelings. Ray, for instance, subconsciously expressed his anger over his unpopularity at school by developing a lean, muscular look that would make him the envy of his classmates. Lori smothered her feelings of frustration by eating huge amounts of food, then used vomiting not only to maintain her weight, but as a symbolic means of getting rid of resentment she did not know how to express in healthier ways.

HOME ENVIRONMENT

For many teens, family structure and function play a part in the development of an eating disorder. In early studies of teens with anorexia nervosa, evidence indicated that parents—particularly overcontrolling mothers—were the primary cause of the disorder. But more and more, experts see disordered teens coming from homes that are safe, loving, and supportive, where parents give their children independence and try their best to build self-esteem and promote happiness.

Even in such homes, however, subtle family influences can push an at-risk teen into an eating disorder. In some cases an overemphasis on food or a parent's preoccupation with size and weight, plays a role. At other times, a teen's mistaken notion of what his or her parent thinks or expects contributes to an eating problem. Ray says, "I always thought my parents expected great things from me, and subconsciously I'd resented them for that. Funny thing, it turned out I was mistaken. All they wanted was for me to be happy."

Unsatisfied Needs

Teens who develop eating disorders usually have many unsatisfied needs that a parent may not even suspect. Some needs are serious and deserve attention, while others may have been brushed aside by parents or teachers as unimportant but persist in the teens' minds. Since they are unable to cope with such problems in better ways, they turn to food to express their frustration.

Teens who have been abused, hurt, or disillusioned often use food to comfort themselves, to numb emotional pain, or to avoid intimacy. For others, their eating disorder is a cry for attention; they are in families that are too busy to notice their emotional needs, or they are at a time in their lives when they lack friends and feel lonely and worthless. "Everyone told me that college was going to be the best years of my life," says Michael, "but it was more like hell. And there was no one I could turn to. No one seemed to notice."

For some teens, their eating disorder is a means of expressing anger or rebellion against parents or some other authority—they eat angrily and voraciously or refuse to eat at all. In this way they exert their own power and control while avoiding direct confrontation with what they perceive to be an uncontrollable problem. Some teens lack a purpose or can't find meaning in life and use an eating disorder to fill empty time, while others find that it gives drama to their lives. "Having an eating disorder made me like a tragic hero in a book," Michael explains. "I didn't drop out of school because I was scared, but because I had a serious illness. A unique illness. In a weird way, I loved the attention it brought me, even though I was totally miserable."

BIOLOGICAL FACTORS

Depression
Many teens who suffer from eating disorders also suffer from depression. Such depression is different from "the blues"—everyday, temporary sadness—or grief that one experiences after the death of a loved one. Those who suffer from sadness or grief usually continue to function in a normal fashion and recover in a short period of time. Severe depression, on the other hand, dramatically affects a teen's mood, thinking, bodily functions, and behavior and often responds only to outside help.

Mood. Teens who suffer from depression show signs of irritability, worry, and/or loss of interest in activities that once gave them pleasure. They have difficulty concentrating and remembering things and have problems making decisions. They often feel hopeless or even suicidal.

Bodily Functions. Many depressed teens suffer from loss of appetite, while others eat compulsively and put on weight. Fatigue, lack of energy, and insomnia are common complaints, although some teens try to escape from their depression by sleeping all the time. At times, depression may take the form of unexplained pains in different parts of the body.

Behavior Changes. Some depressed teens are unable to carry out simple daily activities such as getting dressed or going to school. Many make a great effort to function as normally as possible but admit that they are often unaware of what is going on around them.

Experts are unclear about the exact cause of depression, although they know that it can stem from a variety of factors. Sometimes a specific event—such as a death—can act as a trigger, while at other times the condition seems to appear out of nowhere. External events such as loneliness, worries about school, a breakup with a boyfriend or girlfriend, or leaving home can bring on depression. People from families with a history of depression are more vulnerable. In such cases, experts believe that changes in hormones and certain brain chemicals, called neurotransmitters, may be responsible for the condition. Illnesses, medications, and substances such as alcohol and other drugs are chemical factors that can also cause depression.

Depression is a common side effect of an eating disorder, but many eating-disordered teens were depressed earlier in their lives as well. Such depression and the accompanying feeling of anxiety—a sense of dread that something unspecified but terrible is going to happen—contribute to a negative outlook on life. In addition, these feelings sap energy and motivation and make fears seem overwhelming and insurmountable. "I couldn't focus, much less make good decisions," says Marcella, who battled depression after the death of her brother.

Obsessive and Compulsive Tendencies

In addition to being depressed, teens with eating disorders are often obsessive and compulsive, traits that make it extremely difficult for them to control the urge to diet, binge, or purge. Obsessions are recurring anxious thoughts that are difficult or impossible to put aside, while compulsions are driving needs to act on one's obsession in order to reduce the anxiety. Some teens may be obsessed with a fear of germs or a fear of people and thus will feel compelled to bathe repeatedly or to stay in the house all the time. Eating-disordered teens are obsessed with food and appearance and focus compulsively on eating and dieting. Kathy, who not only washed her hands repeatedly but was obsessed with neatness, made progress overcoming her bingeing and purging after she began taking antidepressants, which helped control the urges she experienced. "The antidepressants took a while to work, but then I could feel the clouds of anxiety lift. It was like seeing the sun again after a long stormy time. I felt happier, more at peace. The medicine made it easier for me to resist the urge to binge."

SOCIAL FACTORS

Social Pressures to Be Thin

Social pressures that are constant and contradictory appear to be partly responsible for the increasing numbers of eating-disordered adolescents. Our world is obsessed with thinness. Many models and movie stars are angular and emaciated. Magazines are filled with weight-reduction plans and diet tips. Health experts encourage everyone to exercise and cut out the fat in foods. The idea seems to be that, with the right diet, exercise, shampoo, and makeup, we can all attain the perfect body—tall, thin, taut, and tanned—and the perfect look.

Teens in America grow up with such messages and incorporate them into their outlook. People, however, come in all shapes and sizes, and most teens cannot achieve the body of a model no matter how hard they try. Nevertheless, they do try and, in the process, grow extremely frustrated and unhappy with their bodies and themselves. Studies show that more than 60 percent of

Models, who are generally thinner than average, seem to set the standard for the ideal, although unrealistic, body type. This can put tremendous pressure on a teen with low self-esteem. Kate Moss, for example, was one of the most popular supermodel icons of the 1990s.

female high-school students believe they are overweight, when in fact less than 20 percent really are. A 1996 survey showed that young girls fear becoming overweight more than they worry about cancer, nuclear war, or losing their parents. Another study showed that almost 90 percent of seventeen-year-old girls and almost 50 percent of nine-year-old girls are on diets, while girls as young as five and six worry about being too heavy.

Social Pressures to Eat

At the same time that society worships thinness, teens are under tremendous social pressure to eat. Many parents teach their children that it is wrong to waste food and rude to refuse food offered by another adult. Television commercials endlessly push tantalizing products and link eating with happiness, popularity, and fun. Restaurants and fast-food chains lure patrons with mouthwatering specials that are often twice the size of a normal meal. As one author observes, "For teens, the contradictory messages to eat and still be thin are confusing and impossible to follow. Yet some kids who don't know how to face the really difficult issues of life let themselves be sidetracked by conflicts over food and appearance."

Social Pressures to Achieve

The status of women in modern society has improved, but along with new opportunities have come increased pressures on women to compete, achieve, and succeed. What was meant to be a liberating philosophy has in reality become a demanding one. Working outside the home, women are expected to be intelligent, assertive, independent, and extremely competent. At the same time, many maintain their traditional roles as wives and mothers who throw lavish birthday parties, carpool kids to Little League practice, and sew costumes for class plays. They want to have time for their husbands, to nurture their children, to keep a clean house, and to put a home-cooked meal on the table. When such proves impossible, they feel frustrated. "My mom's an accomplished professional and works full-time outside the home," Lori says, "but she puts a high priority on having spotless bathrooms. When the chrome doesn't shine, she fusses. I don't get it."

After watching their mothers struggle, it is no wonder that teenage girls are often confused and overwhelmed when they try to decide what to do with their own lives. The choices are challenging and sometimes contradictory. Many young women with poor self-esteem or an unrealistic view of life are afraid to face those challenges and retreat into an eating disorder, which allows them to appear weak and ill and postpones any need to make a decision about their future.

WHAT ARE THE TRIGGERS FOR AN EATING DISORDER?

Although it can be difficult to pinpoint the "start" of an eating disorder, often there is a precipitating event—something that triggers the onset of the illness. A trigger can be words, looks, or even situations. For Ray, it was the accident that prevented him from exercising. Liz disliked the curves she developed when she went through puberty. "I gained weight, and in our house that was a bad thing. Besides that, I'd lost control of my body, and that was scary."

Teachers and Classes

Despite the best of intentions, teachers can inadvertently trigger eating disorders. For instance, a health teacher might schedule "fat testing" in her class, forgetting that the practice encourages size comparisons and can be emotionally devastating to teens who are already worried about being overweight. "I had a cooking teacher who was very outspoken about not wanting anorexics in her classes, and one girl left," says Hannah's sister. "I'm sure the teacher didn't realize how hurtful her comments were. But the last thing someone with an eating disorder needs is to be rejected."

Environmental conservation and animal-rights presentations in social-studies classes also put some students at risk for anorexia, since teens who want to cut calories from their diets have an excuse to do so by becoming vegetarians. Most vegetarians are not anorexic, but vegetarian teens make food their focus and follow a regimen that defines certain types of foods as "forbidden." Like anorexics, some vegetarians suffer from fatigue, depression, malnutrition, and underweight when they do not take the time to learn what to substitute for the products they give up.

Coaches and Sports

Participation in sports and athletics may trigger eating disorders, particularly if a coach is willing to overlook or encourage dysfunctional eating to have a winning team. Dance instructors as well as track, gymnastics, and wrestling coaches often require participants to be extremely lean in order to be successful. Coping with constant hunger, excessive training, and the stress of performance leads to frustration, despair, and guilt that set many vulnerable teens on the road to an eating disorder.

Hollywood and Glamour

For many young teens, something as simple as watching a movie or reading a magazine can trigger an eating disorder. Girls who admire and want to copy the seemingly sophisticated look of bone-thin female stars are often willing to try anything to achieve a desired degree of slenderness. But many ordinary girls are not born with the lean physique of a model, and most lack the resources— money, dietitians, and personal trainers—and the enormous drive that help many in the entertainment industry stay so lean. "No one tells these girls that their favorite

Christy Henrich was one of the top two gymnasts in the United States in 1989. At the age of fifteen the 4-foot-11-inch (150-centimeter), 90-pound (41-kilogram) teen was told by a gymnastics judge that she would never make the Olympic team if she did not lose weight. Christy took his advice to heart and began a diet that soon took over her life. She lost weight—38 pounds (17 kilograms)—and died on July 26, 1994, at the age of twenty-two of multiple organ failure associated with anorexia. Her dreams of becoming an Olympic contestant remained tragically unfulfilled.

stars smoke like chimneys or take drugs or starve themselves in order to maintain that 'beautiful' persona," says one counselor. "I believe eating disorders are more prevalent these days because many young women can't be thin enough without going to harmful lengths to keep off the weight."

Diets

Diets are the most common triggers for eating disorders. One specialist says: "Eating disorders should be called dieting disorders, because it is the dieting process and not eating that causes the initiation of both anorexia and bulimia nervosa."

Going on a diet and losing weight initially give teens more self-confidence as well as a feeling of power and control. When they stop dieting, however, and their weight begins to increase, feelings of frustration and despair can be overpowering. These feelings often lead to another diet, and the teen falls into a cycle of eating and dieting with feelings of self-worth swinging up and down like the needle of a scale. Anorexics break this cycle by restricting food until the thought of eating a normal meal is too terrifying to contemplate. Bulimics, on the other hand, discover that purging is an unpleasant but effective method that allows them to eat as much as they want without gaining weight at all.

Relationships

People with whom teens interact often serve as triggers for anorexia, bulimia, and binge eating. Sexually abusive friends or family members are particularly harmful, as are parents who are overly critical or verbally abusive. A parent's divorce or remarriage can throw a teen's life out of kilter. So can the death of a loved one or the birth of a sibling.

Some triggers are less dramatic, however. Even a casual remark can devastate teens who rely on the approval of others to boost their self-esteem. "I knew one bulimic whose boyfriend told her she ought to go on a diet," a counselor relates. "A more confident girl would probably have just told him where to get off, but for this one, the suggestion was all the motivation she needed."

While eating disorders serve to protect teens from hurtful relationships, they also distance them from friends and loved ones who would like to help. The role that parents, teachers, and friends play in the development of eating disorders and in a teen's recovery is discussed in greater detail in the next chapter.

Chapter Four

RELATIVES AND RELATIONSHIPS

Kathy's Story

*Ancestry played a significant role in the develop-
ment of Kathy's anorexia nervosa, which started
when she was about fifteen. There had been inci-
dents of depression, alcoholism, and suicide on
both sides of her family, and from an early age
Kathy had experienced periods of despondency.
"She was always obedient, but she had a little
frowny face," her parents remember. Like her
parents, Kathy was a perfectionist, but she was
compulsive as well, arranging knickknacks pre-
cisely, then becoming severely upset when they
were moved. "When she was in elementary school,
she went through a stage when she washed her
hands all the time," her mother recalls.*

*Of average size, Kathy had a round face and
had been teased about it when she was young.*

"Even my mother joked about it now and then," Kathy says. *"I know she didn't mean it to be cruel, but I felt bad just the same."*

Her parents were more concerned with achievement than looks, however. An unemotional, hardworking couple, they encouraged their children to do everything well even if that involved sacrifice. At the same time they sent silent messages that one coped with disappointment and failure by hiding feelings and getting on with one's life. Their stoic attitude did not work for Kathy, who was sensitive, emotional, and needed to express herself in more dynamic ways. *"My parents were great, but I guess I got the feeling that they thought emotions were kind of silly. Their attitude seemed to be 'just get on with what's important,'"* she observes.

Kathy's eating disorder was an expression of her inherited emotional characteristics as well as a deep dissatisfaction with herself and her family. Though she was unable to put her feelings into words, she suffered from guilt that she was a *"bad"* daughter, not always able to measure up to their expectations. *"I felt so selfish, like all I did was dwell on my feelings. First I was angry, then guilty, then everything seemed hopeless. Then one day I realized that losing weight was a project that gave my days focus. When the scale was down, I felt good about myself."*

Despite the family's closeness, no one suspected Kathy's problem until a dentist noticed enamel damage during a checkup. The stomach acids she was regularly vomiting were eating away the surface of her teeth.

Shocked, Kathy's parents assumed that dealing with their daughter's illness firmly and *unemotionally would bring about a cure in due time. They began by expressing their disapproval, then moved on to arguing and nagging. When that had no effect, they turned to more extreme measures. Kathy was expected to eat a certain amount of food at each meal. She had to stay at the table until she cleaned her plate. The bathroom was locked after meals to prevent her from going there to purge.*

Showing determination that characterizes many eating-disordered teens, Kathy managed to continue to lose weight anyway. Finally, in desperation, her parents consulted their family minister, who pointed out that they were locked in a power struggle with their daughter. He suggested that they go to an eating-disorder specialist. "All this time, we thought we'd been helping our daughter," Kathy's father says. "If anything, we were making the problem worse. We soon learned that, with eating-disordered kids, you have to look past the obvious—the crazy way they eat—to what's really bugging them. Sometimes, that's you."

EATING DISORDERS AND THE FAMILY

Parents as Role Models

For Kathy and other eating-disordered teens, the makeup of the family and the way it functions are important factors in the development of the disorders. Parents are role models, caregivers, counselors, and, at the best of times, friends. As a teen grows up, however, conflicts are common. Mom and Dad are part of a different generation and often see life from a different perspective. Some parents are neglectful or abusive. Others are caring but overcontrolling.

Since parents are such powerful influences, teens often "buy into" the messages of their parents even when they are not really comfortable with such messages. "Dad always thought he knew what was best for me," Kathy says. "He always had an opinion—what classes I should take, when and where I should go to college, what I might like to major in. I got used to doing what he said, but deep down I guess I was pretty unhappy about it."

Many teens have trouble reconciling the messages they receive from their parents with those they receive from society. "Parents say it pays to study hard, to be honest and hardworking, and to put emphasis on inner values rather than looks," Kathy points out. "From what I see— not that I do this—kids who know how to work the system, who put off doing homework to go to a party, who get the answers from someone in class the next day, and make an A on the test, they do okay, too. What my parents said didn't always make sense."

Some teens cope with this kind of confusion by rebelling. Some are conscientious and want to please others and will suppress the confusion and anger they feel but develop an eating disorder in response. "I wish somebody had explained all this stuff to me sooner," Kathy says. "Although maybe it wouldn't have made a lot of difference. When you're twelve or thirteen, you kind of go with your emotions. If they're confused, you are, too."

The Power of Unspoken Messages

Even in the best of families, unspoken parental messages can influence the development of an eating disorder in a vulnerable teen. A mother who accompanies her expressions of love or sympathy with cookies and milk may unwittingly influence her children to eat every time they are unhappy or lonely. A parent's enthusiasm for jogging or fitness may be interpreted as a prejudice against fat.

Kathy's mother failed to take into account how behavior she considered normal might be interpreted by her daughter. "I dieted off and on throughout Kathy's life," she says. "I didn't think about how it might be affecting her."

Even a parent's positive messages can be misinterpreted by teens whose negative mind-set leads them to expect criticism and rejection. Parents who compliment their children's intelligence by saying "You can accomplish anything you want" may spark the reaction "They expect me to achieve great things." Teens who are shaky about their self-worth may be convinced that they can never live up to such high expectations and may abuse food either to rebel against the pressure or as a way to be or appear less capable. "Developing an eating disorder gave me an excuse to drop out of college and come home," Michael points out. "I know Dad was embarrassed and disappointed, but he couldn't really blame me. After all, I was sick."

Many parents fail to understand the power of the messages they unintentionally communicate to their children. Kathy's father observes: "I guess we were teaching Kathy that it was wrong to show emotion when we played down things like her upsets over a poor grade or two. At the time, I didn't understand how that could hurt her. After all, I'd been raised the same way, and I'd turned out fine."

Unspoken messages are easily misunderstood, since they are not put into words, let alone discussed. For instance, a daughter may interpret her parents' worries about her coming home late as "She is untrustworthy" or "She is not capable of being on her own." In fact, her parents may see their daughter as perfectly capable but are thinking of the dangers posed by drunk drivers or others during late-night hours.

Clearing up nonverbal misunderstandings can be difficult, since neither parent nor child may recognize or admit that a problem exists. Teens may subconsciously use different kinds of communication—temper tantrums, experimentation with drugs, disordered eating patterns—in response. Michael says: "I was basically saying to my parents, 'The way you raised me didn't work. I'm mad, and I'm going to get back at you.' But I hadn't been raised to say stuff like that out loud. It took a lot of time in counseling for me to understand that."

Influence of Conservative Parents
Parents who strictly enforce family or societal rules, who hold conservative values, and who discourage children from expressing their thoughts and feelings often contribute to the development of eating disorders. Such parents commonly assume dominant roles (the father is "head of the house," for example), while children are expected to conform to adult expectations.

Teens in this type of family often grow up lacking communication skills and the ability to tackle and resolve conflicts. They often lack assertiveness and self-confidence after having taken subordinate roles all their lives. "No one in our house argued with Dad," Kathy says. "We were a polite family, and 'talking back' was considered rude."

Influence of Achievement-Oriented Parents
Parents who emphasize success and achievement rather than personal development often set their children up for an eating disorder. In such homes, teens are expected to set high goals for themselves and achieve them at any cost. They are expected to do well in everything they try and usually receive the full support of their parents in their every effort. While it appears—and parents may

think—that they are nurturing their teens by attending every school activity, helping with homework, taking them to music lessons, and encouraging them to take part in sports and other activities, they may in fact be satisfying their own need to be perfect.

Achievement-oriented parents, who communicate their attitudes to their children at every turn, often extend their expectations to include manners and expect their children to be perfectly polite, helpful, tolerant, and loving. In such an atmosphere teens get the message that doubts, fears, and ordinary human failings are unacceptable. Those who feel they cannot measure up to their parents' expectations, or who are fearful and angry but cannot express such emotions, often let their feelings out by developing an eating disorder.

Influence of Critical Parents

Highly critical parents can also prime teens for trouble, since criticism damages self-esteem and promotes a negative outlook on life. It can motivate children to become perfectionists and to believe that nothing they ever do is good enough. They may eventually rebel against the negativism, or they may accept it as a true assessment of their abilities and give up. In all cases they become particularly vulnerable for eating disorders. "My father was openly prejudiced against overweight people," Liz explains. "It took me a long time to realize that some of his other criticisms were more subtle. For instance, when I decided to give up horseback riding, he was very much opposed to my decision. He pointed out how much we had invested in it. How much we enjoyed riding together. I felt stupid and selfish deciding to give it up. There was no support for me there."

Influence of Dysfunctional Parents

Neglect, physical and sexual abuse, alcoholism, and drug addiction in families also make adolescents particularly vulnerable to eating disorders. In such homes, teens often become so uncomfortable with rage, physical abuse, and disorder that they suppress and deny their own anger or feelings of confusion and uncertainty. When they have no one to rely on to give them support and love, they grow to fear the future and try to gain control of every aspect of their lives. Food often becomes a source of comfort, and eating is the one activity that can be structured and controlled in an otherwise chaotic and dangerous existence.

Young women in single-parent families who regularly "mother" younger sisters and brothers are at high risk for becoming binge eaters, since they often rely on food as their one pleasure in an unfair, uncaring world. Teens who have been sexually abused often hide behind food. Binge eaters use their size to avoid further sexual relationships and to avoid facing the guilt and shame they feel. Anorexics try to maintain a childlike body and "refuse to grow up." Bulimics try to smother their memories with food, then purge to symbolically get rid of the ugly secrets they harbor.

Effect of Eating Disorders on Parents

Eating disorders not only affect the teens who suffer from them, but have a terrible impact on parents as well. Sitting at a table watching an anorexic daughter take birdlike portions of food; listening to her roam the house at night, bingeing and purging; watching an overweight son come home from school in tears after being teased by his classmates—all are situations that parents of eating-disordered teens face daily. They become frightened, angry, frustrated, and confused. Tensions run high, and other interests go unheeded as they struggle to cope with their child's baffling behavior. "It was almost impossible to eat with Kathy sitting there, scowling at her plate every night," her mother remembers. "We'd all be pretending that everything was all right, but there was a knot the size of a baseball in my throat. After dinner, her father and I would take turns making sure she didn't go to the bathroom. It was like we were guards in a prison. The worst experience I could ever imagine!"

Parents who discover that a child is trapped in a behavior that will not change no matter how much they talk, threaten, cajole, or supervise find themselves torn apart by disagreements and arguments over who is to blame and what to do next. Often the damage is so extensive that they need family or marital counseling to help repair the resulting wounds.

Effect of Eating Disorders on Siblings

Siblings of eating-disordered teens sometimes feel neglected because so much time and energy is devoted to the needs of the disordered sister or brother. To earn attention, siblings frequently adopt their own means of coping, sometimes by taking on the role of "good child," sometimes by rebelling in a different way—drinking, using drugs, doing poorly at school—sometimes by developing an eating disorder themselves.

Kathy's sister chose a less spectacular method. "When Kathy was around, it was like having a bomb in the house, ready to explode. I knew she particularly hated anyone to come into the kitchen when she was there, so I made it a point of going in, you know, just to get a drink of water or something. She'd start yelling, then Mom would hurry in and pull me into the hall and give me a little lecture. For a few minutes at least, I had her complete attention."

EATING DISORDERS AND PEERS

Relationships with Peers

Since social life and relationships are very important to teens, peer pressure from friends and classmates can play a significant role in the development of an eating disorder.

Most teens want nothing more than to fit in and to be accepted. They strictly follow accepted styles of appearance and behavior within their particular group and are strongly influenced by movies and television shows that are popular with their friends. Any change in their own size and shape can be a source of anxiety and concern. "I worried about all kinds of things besides my face," Kathy says. "I was afraid I was too serious, that my hair didn't shine enough, that my boobs were too big, that my jeans made me look heavy. Everyone worried about those things. I just took my worries too far."

Parents who laugh off such concerns do not understand or have forgotten the strength of peer pressure that teens face. Not only does being plain, out of style, or overweight usually carry the stigma of being stupid, inferior, and rejected, but studies show that some children link overweight with cheating and lying as well. And at a time when discrimination against any minority group is not tolerated, size prejudice is alive and well. "Some of the nicest people I know are disgusted by someone who's fat," Marcella says. "They assume we're lazy—the kind of people who leave tons of dirty dishes in the sink and scatter Twinkie wrappers all over the house."

Influence of Girlfriends

Teenage girls exert significant pressure on one another to pay attention to appearance, worry about weight, and even to eat dysfunctionally. Girls often become concerned with their weight in elementary school, and "going on a diet" is now a rite of passage among preteens. "It seemed like every popular girl was on a diet when I was in fifth grade." Hannah remembers. "Of course I wanted to go on one, too. I was mad when my mom said 'no.' I felt left out; like they were all grown up and I was stuck being a fat little girl."

As they grow older, young women come under increased pressure from one another to think about their

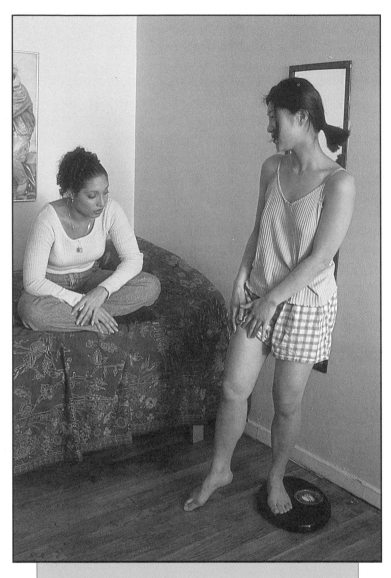

Teenage girls are constantly exposed to the views of their peers, the majority of whom buy into society's message that a girl must diet and try to be thin if she wants to be beautiful, successful, and happy.

weight. They may seldom associate with members of an older generation who have a different perspective and different priorities when it comes to appearance and nutrition. Hannah points out: "We'd all sit around the cafeteria table, talking about our weight, skipping meals, moaning about how much we'd eaten and how we were getting fat. It was like a club or something."

Influence of Boyfriends

Young men often unwittingly put pressure on girls to be thin. "In social studies we learned that men used to like curvy women," Kathy says. "But I think things are changing. Young movie stars aren't built like Marilyn Monroe anymore. The female leads that guys see on TV and in movies today are skinny. And at school, the skinny girls seem to have a lot of confidence. Why shouldn't the guys be attracted to them?"

Programmed by our culture that thin is beautiful, many boys gravitate to girls who are slender and "sexy." Overweight girls are often teased, insulted, and scorned by their male classmates. So powerful is the need to be accepted by the opposite sex that a boy's casual remark that a girl ought to "lose a few pounds" can be crushing enough to trigger an eating disorder. Many girls believe that their chances of dating or developing a relationship with a boy are poor unless they keep their weight within an acceptable range.

Influence of Males on Males

Just as young women feel pressure to be thin, more and more young men are pushing themselves to be firm and muscular. Skinny or undersized boys are often left out or teased about their size. Boys who are overweight face size prejudice, which can destroy their social life and crush their self-esteem.

The lean body of the long-distance runner has become an ideal for many young men. So has the "inverted triangle" torso of the bodybuilder or body sculptor. Young men who work out in such sports often emphasize competition and appearance rather than health. Without understanding how it happens, many find that their interest has become an obsession and that they have developed an eating disorder somewhere along the way to becoming fit.

RESOLVING CONFLICT

Once an eating disorder develops, changing a teen's focus from appearance and food to more worthwhile internal values can take years of therapy and hard work. Resolving conflict is easier, however, if friends and family do their part to help.

Counseling can shine light on troubled interactions, such as unspoken rules that create anxiety or anger, improper reactions to stress, or the use of food to express love. Parents can benefit from counseling to learn the best way to help their daughter or son. "We learned that focusing on Kathy's low weight was one of the worst things we could do," explains her parents. "Her eating habits became off limits for family discussions. Instead, we focused on changes we needed to make—letting her be more independent, make her own decisions, and hardest of all, make her own mistakes."

Friends, too, need to educate themselves regarding the underlying reasons for eating disorders, so that they can be sensitive to the needs of someone who is eating dysfunctionally. "Girls who find out that a friend has an eating disorder often make a big fuss and try to make her eat," points out one counselor. "All of which plays right into her focus on food and her craving for attention."

A teen needs the right kind of understanding and support in order to recover from an eating disorder. The following points can be used as guidelines to help ensure that no one unwittingly encourages a troubled teen in his or her dysfunctional behavior.

- *Evaluate and understand attitudes about weight, size, and appearance.* Do you criticize people who are overweight? Do you link appearance and worth? Are you an emotional eater? When dealing with an eating-disordered teen, try not to use food as a socializing agent, since it then becomes tied even more strongly to emotions. Try not to make comments on appearance, either good or bad, and remember that messages can be nonverbal. You may not openly nag or criticize, but your facial expressions or body language may be conveying a negative message. "After I put on weight, Dad used to frown when I took a second helping of spaghetti," Ray remembers. "Even without words, his disapproval came through loud and clear, believe me."

- *Avoid scare tactics and power struggles.* Eating-disordered individuals are already frightened and dealing with feelings of inadequacy and unhappiness. Impatience, threats, and anger may push them deeper into their disorder. "I basically tuned my parents out when they started criticizing my eating," Kathy says. "Deep inside, though, I was determined that they weren't going to win this one. The more they talked, the more important it seemed that I win."

  Don't prepare or buy special food for disordered teens. Kindly but firmly insist that they take charge of their own eating and their own behavior, including cleaning the kitchen and bathroom after use and replacing food that has been used for bingeing.

- *Do not ignore the disorder.* Although eating-disordered teens may deny that they have a problem, parents in particular need to be prepared to help by finding a treatment program that works. Allow the teen to have some say in choosing the treatment, and be prepared to go into family counseling. Don't forget regular medical and dental checkups to fend off physical problems, and if the disorder becomes life-threatening, be prepared to intervene and get the teen to a doctor or hospital as soon as possible.

- *Maintain other interests.* Despite concern for a disordered teen's health and safety, family and friends need to maintain other interests as well. Go to the movies. Get involved in community activities. If necessary, parents can find a safe place for the disordered teen to stay so that the rest of the family can go on vacation or enjoy a day at the beach. Such activities will not only provide a break from tension but also allow the teen to see that there are things in life other than his or her illness. Good communication and time spent with others will also go far to prevent the development of additional problems such as depression, marital discord, or eating disorders among friends or siblings.

- *Be patient.* Eating-disordered teens, especially those who are very thin or who binge and purge several times a day, are seriously ill and cannot always think or respond clearly to logical arguments or discussions. Rather, they need encouragement to continue to try to overcome their disorder and support during the long, difficult process of restoring their minds and bodies to health.

The process of recovery may take years. There will be relapses, and some individuals never recover completely. Fortunately, the variety and effectiveness of treatment options are growing as experts gain greater understanding of these illnesses. The following chapter will explain the most widely used treatments, as well as the goals that experts aim for as they work to help eating-disordered teens reestablish healthy lifestyles.

Chapter Five

GETTING HELP

Liz's Story

Liz grew up in a large family and had a good relationship with her parents, although it was based more on shared activities than on friendship and emotional closeness. While growing up, Liz shared her father's love of horses, but when she turned fourteen, she decided to give up riding for other interests—after-school sports, baby-sitting, shopping, and boys. Her father was openly angry about her decision, and their relationship changed for the worse. As a result, Liz felt terribly guilty. Inasmuch as she had experienced bouts of depression since the age of seven or eight, it was natural that she became depressed as well.

Adolescence was a difficult time for Liz. She changed almost overnight from a shapeless little girl to one of the tallest and curviest young women in her class. The weight she gained at this time bothered her a lot, since her father was openly critical of her mother's heaviness. Dieting was acceptable in her family—her mother dieted periodically but unsuccessfully—so Liz went on several "healthy" diets with her parents' blessing. She ate plenty of fruits and vegetables, limited calories to less than 800 a day, and lost weight. Always being hungry was frustrating, however, and after six months of gnawing hunger, she turned to a friend for help. "I knew she could make herself throw up whenever she wanted to, so I just asked her how she did it," Liz remembers.

Self-induced vomiting was "really disgusting" at first, but Liz soon grew to rely on it and even turned to other methods to continue to lose weight. She spent all her baby-sitting money on laxatives and diet pills. When she ran short of cash, she shoplifted what she needed. "I felt really, really bad doing it, since I'd always considered myself a basically honest person. But I had to—I had to keep bingeing and purging. If I tried to resist, the craving would grow until I couldn't think of anything else."

Liz's mother, a nurse, naturally was concerned when she realized that her daughter seemed to be going too far with dieting. The reassurances of their family doctor, who did not bother to ask Liz about her eating habits, failed to calm her fears. She noted that Liz had many symptoms of anorexia nervosa. She always wore loose, layered clothing, was growing fine downy lanugo hair on her arms, and was no longer menstruating. She always seemed to be cold and even slept under two electric blankets at night. "Then I happened to get a glimpse of her naked. That was the

83

clincher," Liz's mother says. "I confronted her; we had a battle royal, and she admitted to what she'd been doing. I took her back to the doctor the next day."

Faced with the facts, the family physician agreed to admit Liz to an inpatient eating-disorder unit at the hospital in order to stabilize her weight and electrolytes, which had been upset by purging. Treatment followed a traditional, but largely ineffective, approach that forced a patient to eat but ignored the psychological reasons for the disorder. Liz gained a few pounds, but that only made her more angry and anxious. Outwardly passive and compliant, she surprised everyone when she took the initiative and checked herself out of treatment a few days later. "No one was going to force me to gain weight. Mom and Dad threatened to kick me out of the house if I didn't stay in counseling, but I knew they were bluffing. I wasn't eighteen yet. They were too scared to let me go out on my own." Still, Liz reluctantly agreed to see a counselor and conscientiously kept every appointment, even though, like others who are in treatment involuntarily, she resisted making any changes.

With the help of her counselor, Liz managed to wean herself off laxatives over the next few months but made no further progress. She still vomited regularly and continued to steal diuretics and food. Finally, the inevitable happened. She was caught shoplifting, and the police were called in. Unfortunately, her parents were not notified, so Liz was released to face her fear, shame, and self-loathing alone.

To punish herself, she set about a course of excessive bingeing and purging that lasted for hours. Finally, her malnourished and abused body collapsed, and she suffered a heart attack. Medics rushed her to the hospital, where Liz returned to consciousness to face her angry father and distraught mother. "We both wanted the best for Liz, but we couldn't agree whether that meant being there for her or cutting her loose—letting her sink or swim, so to speak," says her mother. "Finally the counselor stepped in. She agreed that Liz needed help, but pointed out that our differences were hampering our daughter's recovery and suggested that marriage counseling might be in order. It was a shock, but we agreed."

THE SEARCH FOR TREATMENT

Obtaining an Accurate Diagnosis

Not long ago, eating-disordered teens and their parents found that treatment was hard to find. Primary-care physicians often did not understand the underlying causes of the disorders and elected to put their overweight patients on diets while telling anorexics and bulimics to "just stop" their self-destructive behaviors.

Teens can and do recover from an eating disorder without help, but their numbers are small. Without treatment, they are likely to continue harmful behaviors, which become more ingrained and difficult to change as time passes. Their physical health usually deteriorates, and permanent damage to their bones, brain, heart, digestive tract, and other organs results. "Expecting an eating-disordered teen to stop restricting calories, bingeing, or purging is like expecting a snowstorm in midsummer," says one expert. "It happens, but rarely. You don't count on it."

Although parents of disordered teens must be alert for professionals who are misguided, poorly informed, or self-serving (or even in the throes of an eating disorder themselves), they can be encouraged that health-care workers have gained a better knowledge of eating disorders. Many doctors are aware of the emotional as well as physical problems suffered by eating-disordered patients. Qualified counselors and therapists, who have been trained to deal with both the physical and emotional aspects of the problem, are easier to find. A growing number of organizations exist throughout the United States to educate and guide those who need more information.

Accepting the Diagnosis

When entering treatment, binge eaters have no trouble accepting a diagnosis of their disorder, since they are well aware of their problems and are eager to find a way to end dysfunctional eating. Once in therapy, however, they may resist treatment, since counselors usually advise that they give up dieting, and the thought can be extremely frightening.

Anorexics and bulimics, who are often forced by parents to enter therapy, commonly resist treatment as well. Some are outwardly rebellious. Most appear compliant but are seething with rage. Some stall, make excuses, and put off going until they are critically ill. At this point, these people may need to be hospitalized, supervised, and force-fed so that their weight and other body functions can stabilize.

Hospitalized anorexics and bulimics will often fight hard against a return to normal eating since all are afraid that, if they give up their present dysfunctional ways of controlling their weight, they will get fat. Hospital personnel must be on the watch for their stratagems to get rid of unwanted calories. Patients may give food to other patients, hide it in flowerpots, flush it down toilets, or throw it out of windows. Some who are made to eat hold the food in their mouth until they can spit it out or will

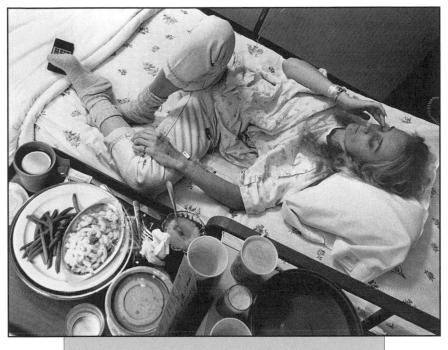

Since severe malnutrition and extremely low body weight affect a person's ability to think clearly, hospitalized anorexics must often gain weight before the psychotherapy or counseling phase

sneak out of bed and exercise vigorously to burn off the calories they have taken in. "I know of a patient who punched a hole in the wall and stuffed food in there," remembers one nurse. "Her trick fell through when the food began to smell, though."

Choosing a Counselor or Therapist

Starting treatment is a frightening step for anyone with an eating disorder. Most are afraid to face the conflicts that caused the disorder. Many insist that they have no such conflicts. All fear entering the unknown, especially putting their lives in the hands of a stranger.

It is important that each patient find a therapist or counselor who is caring and concerned, understands individual needs, and believes that recovery is possible. He or she should be a licensed mental-health professional who is fully trained in diagnosis, can recognize when symptoms of mental disorders might be due to physical causes, and has an extensive background in dealing with eating disorders. In some cases, a counselor may have recovered from an eating disorder or may have a child who has suffered from an eating disorder and will thus have greater empathy for the patient's feelings.

In all cases, counselors must be a combination of confidant, instructor, mentor, and guide. They must be able to help clients recognize that they have problems. They must help them sort through the tangle of thoughts and feelings that led to their disorder. They must encourage them to learn new ways to deal with the world and the people in it.

"My counselor helped me look at things from other points of view," Kathy explains. "She had confidence in me, believed in me, and accepted me for who I was. Sometimes she said things that were hard for me to take, but that got me to thinking—sometimes even to arguing. I never had to worry about upsetting her, though, and I never had to pretend around her. I could say anything without fear."

TREATMENT AND THERAPY

Therapists often use a variety of treatments and therapies to help their clients recover from their eating disorders. Work begins with preliminary assessment, followed by cognitive, behavioral, interpersonal, and nutritional counseling, which are usually used simultaneously throughout the course of therapy. In this way, clients can begin to improve their physical health as they explore the inner causes of their illness.

Preliminary Assessment

In the first stage of treatment, the therapists attempt to learn as much as possible about the eating disorder, how it has progressed over time, and if the client is using it to escape from a demanding world, to rebel against authority, to release tension, or for some other reason. They learn the client's eating habits—the restrictions, rituals, quantity and type of foods eaten, and triggers for bingeing and purging. They find out how the client feels about herself, her body, her friends and family, and her world. They also encourage the client to talk about feelings, since many clients have never examined their emotions before and have difficulty putting them into words.

ESTABLISHING A TREATMENT PLAN

After establishing a relationship, therapists will use all they have learned to recommend a treatment plan. They might suggest that the client take medication to ease depression and anxiety. They may provide reading material on eating disorders, as well as suggest that clients keep a journal of their thoughts and feelings. Many therapists also ask their clients to keep a food journal to identify food habits and problems.

Some therapists see family therapy as essential at this point and work with parents to fully understand the teen's background and to help stabilize the home environment. Overall, a treatment plan usually involves hours of talking interspersed with activities such as list-making, role-playing, assertiveness training, and art therapy. Together, therapist, client, and sometimes parents explore the client's disordered way of thinking toward finding a remedy.

Often, when teens find themselves in a peaceful, nonconfrontational setting, they are more willing to admit that the eating disorder is not a satisfactory solution to their problems. Liz says, "I wasn't happy doing things my way. I'd gotten to the point of wanting to die. It finally got through to me—my way wasn't working. Maybe I should give my counselor's way a try."

Cognitive Therapy

Cognitive therapy, which focuses on how one thinks and feels, is used by therapists to help disordered teens change the misconceptions they have about themselves. The process, which can stretch over months or years, involves getting teens to understand the reasons for their disordered eating, to recognize their negative beliefs and thought processes, and to substitute positive, realistic statements for erroneous ones.

In cognitive therapy, clients are helped to identify their internal strengths and talents, rebuild their poor self-esteem, and modify their "black-and-white" thinking. They are also encouraged to identify things they enjoy that are not related to food.

"I had the hardest time coming up with something I wanted to do as opposed to what I thought I needed to do," Liz explains. "I'd come up with something—like going to a movie—and then I'd find all these reasons why I shouldn't. I might not enjoy it. I'd be spending too much money. Deep down inside, I guess I didn't believe I deserved to have fun."

Behavioral Therapy

Behavioral therapy is based on the need to change self-destructive behaviors involved in eating disorders. This type of therapy focuses as much on doing as on thinking. Teens make lists of situations that trigger dysfunctional eating and decide on strategies to avoid such situations. They write down everything they eat during the course of the day with notes on how they felt when they ate it. They work on strategies for coping with the stress that often leads to disordered eating and may choose to go for a walk, write a letter, or work on an art project when they feel their emotions begin to rise. They often decide on someone to call for support when they feel like skipping a meal or bingeing and purging.

"My counselor was my safety net until I found someone else I could confide in," says Liz. "In the midst of a crisis, I could call her. I wasn't as nervous tackling my disorder, because I knew she'd always be there with encouragement, a suggestion, something. Just a phone call away."

Interpersonal Therapy

The goal of interpersonal therapy is to help disordered teens improve social skills and work through relationships that are unhealthy or harmful. For instance, teens can be overly dependent on parents or may hate a person who has abused them. They have difficulty controlling anger, impulses, or fluctuations in mood. "After using steroids, I had bad problems with anger and losing my temper," Ray says. "I'm still working on self-control and with getting along better with my folks. I think I've learned some ways to cope. At least I haven't thrown anything for a long time."

Almost all eating-disordered teens have poor social and communication skills and benefit from interpersonal therapy. Treatment usually involves a therapist listening in a nonjudgmental manner, then suggesting strategies to help clients improve their outlook and social skills.

Nutritional Therapy

Nutritional therapy, which sometimes involves the services of a dietitian, helps disordered teens establish healthy eating habits. They work on replacing chaotic eating with more regular patterns—usually three healthy meals plus two optional snacks a day. They learn about food groups and a balanced diet. The dietitian and/or therapist helps them to slowly reintroduce "feared" foods and to create menus that add calories to strict diets.

Dietitians also work to eliminate misunderstandings and myths about food and eating. For instance, they teach teens that fat should not be entirely eliminated from the diet since many vitamins are fat-soluble and are stored in body fat.

"When learning to make food choices, kids should know that there are no "good" foods, no "bad" foods," writes Frances M. Berg, author of *Afraid to Eat*. "The idea that some foods are healthy and others unhealthy, suggesting that some foods can be used like medicine and others produce disease is false and unscientific, even though it is often promoted in the press, and even by health professionals who fail to understand nutrition."

SETTINGS FOR TREATMENT

Inpatient Clinics and Hospitals

During inpatient treatment, a teen enters an eating-disorder clinic or hospital for a period of time in order to focus on the treatment of the disorder. Often this occurs when the teen is severely depressed, near collapse, or not responding to outpatient care. In such facilities, the teen can be observed and cared for full-time and receive frequent and intensive psychiatric and nutritional counseling. Since the teen probably cannot judge how much to eat, cannot control the desire to purge, or may be too terrified of food to eat at all, meals are planned by the staff and served in supervised surroundings. Inpatient clinics also give distraught family members a chance to relax and gain perspective while their child is safe and well supervised.

Hospitals and inpatient clinics are much more expensive than outpatient therapy; thus, a course of treatment may be short and designed only to stabilize the patient physically. Often no effort is made to change the patient's way of thinking. "I was put in the eating-disorder unit of our hospital at one point," Liz relates, "but there was no counseling, no therapy. I left because they made me gain weight, and I hated it."

Many hospitals lack a unit for eating-disordered patients. Teens are usually placed in a regular ward where the staff may not be aware of their specific needs. Nurses may mistake cooperative behavior as a sign of recovery and not recognize the fact that their patients will use all sorts of devious behavior to avoid gaining weight.

Outpatient Settings

While helpful in some situations, inpatient treatment disrupts teens' education and deprives them of any family and social life they may still enjoy. In outpatient settings, teens who are not critically ill can continue to live at home while meeting with a professional therapist at least once a week. They can also keep appointments with a psychiatrist and a dietitian if such treatments seem warranted.

"Meeting with a therapist once or twice a week after school allows her to retain some privacy," explains one therapist. "If she wants, she can avoid the notoriety of being labeled 'the anorexic' or 'the bulimic' by teachers and schoolmates. It gives her the opportunity to remain, at least in public, a somewhat normal kid."

FREQUENCY AND DURATION OF TREATMENT

Patients involved in inpatient treatment are able to take part in various types of therapy throughout the day every day. Patients in outpatient treatment usually go for counseling an hour at a time, once or twice a week. "I can't push for more than that," says one counselor. "Any oftener and they get scared. Think they're being pressured into something. Then they don't show up at all."

Duration of treatment is as variable as the eating-disordered clients themselves. On average, it can range from six months for those who are not seriously ill and are motivated to make changes, to five years or more for those with complicating factors. "A lot of times, growing up makes all the difference. Some teens just need the insight and perspective that comes with age," one therapist explains. "Others get tired of their disorder. They get tired of feeling bad all the time. Maybe they're even a little bored with the whole thing. A few get stuck; they may be in therapy indefinitely."

THE NATURE OF THERAPY

Individual Therapy

Therapy for anorexia and bulimia is often restricted to one-on-one sessions between therapist and client, for several reasons. First, the therapist must establish a relationship of trust with the client, and this is usually easier in a private setting. Disordered teens are insecure, reticent, and defensive, all of which contribute to difficulties with communication. Many conceal secrets that they are unwilling to share with family but will communicate to an outsider whom they have come to respect.

Next, since each teen's disorder is unique, treatment must be personalized. A therapist may spend a great deal of time helping one teen resolve family problems but will skip over family to focus on the poor self-esteem and social issues that are important to another.

Finally, individual therapy sidesteps potentially harmful interactions among disordered teens. Most therapists are aware that anorexic and bulimic teens can be very competitive if brought together for therapy. If not handled with great care, group counseling sessions (or the time in the parking lot afterward) can become a time to exchange telephone numbers, information on weight, and tips for bingeing and purging. "I was invited to take part in group counseling sessions for girls with eating disorders when I went to college," Liz says. "But I decided not to get involved. Just thinking about it made me want to lose weight so everyone would know I was 'the best' anorexic. I could feel myself getting competitive in a very bad way."

Group Therapy

As clients make progress in dealing with their eating disorders, a therapist may suggest group sessions in which several people with similar problems meet together regularly to share concerns and insights. Such group sessions are particularly helpful for binge eaters, who benefit from the support of others with similar concerns. For many teens, knowing that there are others who share their problems and feelings can be reassuring and encouraging.

Group therapy is sometimes structured—that is, members follow a definite format with planned lessons and time set aside for sharing. At other times, it is unstructured, with no specific topic or agenda. Groups may be solely for men or women; others may be mixed. Despite their variations, all groups made up of anorexics or bulimics should be supervised by a therapist who makes sure that the group is progressing in the right direction. There is no benefit to members if they compete with one another or discuss new ways to eat dysfunctionally.

Family Therapy

Family therapy is often a necessity when treating eating disorders, since no one in the family is immune to the stress and disruption caused by the illness. Parents are often angry, confused, or feel inadequate to deal with their child. They may feel guilty about their role in causing the problem. They may feel stressed after hiding their child's condition from neighbors and friends for months. They may be fighting with each other over what to do. Siblings may feel ignored and unloved, since so much attention is being paid to the "sick" child. In such cases, family members can benefit from airing their problems in a safe setting and from getting the support and counsel of a trained professional who understands their feelings.

There are other important reasons for family therapy. Parents unwittingly may be contributing to the disorder by their attitudes and behaviors and may need guidance on how to change. In cases of abuse, parents often need to be confronted with the truth and helped to take action. At times, parents need to talk to the therapist about activities in the home—a teen's bingeing and purging all night, eating food that the family cannot afford to replace, etc.—in order to form a plan of action that will lower stress and help restore calm.

Family counseling sessions may be brief or extended. The therapist may sometimes include only the client and siblings, sometimes the client and parents, sometimes only the parents. Progress is usually slow and complex but can allow families to become closer, share secrets, deal with unrealistic expectations, and clear up misunderstandings. "I'd been seeing my folks as 'the enemy,'" Michael remembers. "I hadn't realized that their picking and nagging was a way of expressing concern."

Self-Help Groups

In some instances, self-help groups are beneficial to those with eating disorders. Overeaters Anonymous (OA) and

Family therapy can take many forms and include different combinations of family members since everyone in the family is affected by a teen's eating disorder. Author Barbara Moe writes in *Coping with Eating Disorders*: "Specialists learned long ago that when one person in the family is having trouble, others are probably in trouble, too."

its sister organization Bulimics Anonymous (BA) are two self-help groups that allow members to share their concerns in an uncritical setting, while also providing a network of support for those who are tempted to binge-eat when they are alone. In many self-help groups such as

OA, no therapists are present at meetings. OA's guidelines, however, which are modeled on the twelve-step plan of Alcoholics Anonymous, require that each member acquire a sponsor from the group who can help that member set up healthy eating plans and carry them out. OA and BA members are also encouraged to write out their feelings and problems in order to better understand their reasons for overeating, as well as to contact other members weekly to receive and offer support.

Self-help groups pose some dangers, however. They provide opportunities for teens to meet in unsupervised surroundings and exchange harmful information. They can be so comfortable that teens maintain their disorders in order to remain a part of the group. Since they do not include a professional to regularly assess the well-being of members, a teen's health may deteriorate without anyone noticing the changes.

MEDICATION AS AN AID TO TREATMENT

Antidepressants

There are no medicines that cure eating disorders, but certain new drugs allow doctors to treat accompanying conditions that may undermine a teen's ability to recover fully.

Experts have found that antidepressant medications, which work by increasing the supply of neurotransmitters in the brain to necessary levels, can play an important role in easing depression as well as moderating the mood swings suffered by bulimics. The newest class of antidepressants, known as selective serotonin reuptake inhibitors (SSRIs), are widely known and include Prozac, Paxil, and Zoloft. These have similar levels of effectiveness as earlier antidepressants but present fewer side effects. Antidepressants such as fluvoxamine (Luvox) are proving beneficial in easing symptoms of anxiety and obsession, which are sometimes part of a disordered individual's personality.

Antidepressants, which are inaccurately portrayed on television comedies as "feel-good drugs" that cause instant euphoria, must be taken daily and require several weeks before they take full effect. Individuals who have a mild case of the blues, who are lonely or homesick, or who maintain a pessimistic outlook on life may not notice as much improvement in their outlook as do patients who suffer from depression resulting from a brain chemical deficiency.

Anti-Obesity Drugs

In 1996 the Food and Drug Administration (FDA) approved two anti-obesity drugs: dexfenfluramine, marketed under the name of Redux, and fenfluramine (Pondimin), which when taken with the drug phentermine became the popular combination known as fen-phen. These drugs, which worked on the brain to decrease the appetite, promised to give some aid to overweight persons who had not been able to lose weight before.

The FDA originally declared these drugs safe for short-term use by severely obese individuals at high risk for heart attack, stroke, and other life-threatening illnesses. They quickly became "miracle drugs" for millions of people who just wanted to lose a few pounds. Doctors prescribed them freely but offered little if any information or advice about the importance of behavior modification for permanent weight loss and control.

Shortly after approval by the FDA, Redux and fen-phen were found to cause serious heart-valve damage in a significant number of users. They were removed from the market in September 1997, barely a year after their release. Equally effective drugs with fewer harmful side effects may be offered in the future. One, known as Meridia, is already available.

But none of these drugs replaces the need for exercise and healthy eating, nor do they address the psychological and emotional reasons why people overeat. For binge and compulsive eaters, there can be no substitute for professional therapists and support groups who can provide the help needed to overcome disordered thinking as well as poor eating habits.

GOALS OF RECOVERY

When eating-disordered teens take on the challenge of recovery, they are committing to an enormous task that involves changing harmful eating patterns and modifying the way they view themselves, their friends and family, and the world around them. Eating-disorder specialist Jeanne Phillips spells out the specifics of the task:

> *People with eating disorders must learn to take responsibility for their feelings and behaviors; begin realistic goal-setting; be willing to take risks without being absolutely certain of the outcomes; ask others for help and support; take the words* should *and* can't *out of their vocabulary; realize that recovery is a process and cannot be done perfectly; avoid isolating and withdrawing; not assume what other people are thinking; not gauge their feelings of specialness on external symbols of success; and begin to establish an identity apart from being someone who is bulimic or anorexic.*

Taking Responsibility for Feelings and Behaviors

In order for eating-disordered teens to recover, they must learn to understand and take responsibility for their feelings rather than suppress or deny them as they have for so many years. Blame, which is often a factor in eating disorders, needs to be dealt with as well. "I subconsciously blamed my parents for my eating disorder," Michael explains. "They had raised me 'wrong,' sent me off to college socially unprepared." Lori says, "Rational or not, I blamed my parents for passing on the genes that made me a big girl." And Hannah adds, "For me, it was God. I'm past that now, but I blamed Him for my depression, my obsessiveness, and my pessimistic outlook."

When teens in counseling gain the skills to take charge of the way they think and behave, they are better able to make the changes and improvements necessary to recover from their dysfunctional eating.

Realistic Goal-Setting

Realistic goal-setting is another objective for eating-disordered teens, since their perfectionism, black-and-white thinking, and negative mind-set often lead them to expect too much or too little of themselves. "I remember being so depressed, hardly able to get out of bed in the morning, and telling myself I should be happy and fun-loving and easygoing," Liz remembers. "Of course, I couldn't live up to that, and I was devastated. Now I know that if I get up on time, am polite to my family at the breakfast table, and maybe find a couple of things to smile about during the course of the day, I'm doing the best I can."

Taking Risks

"Trying something that I might fail at is still unbelievably hard," says Hannah. "When I have to take on a new project in school, I'm convinced I'm going to fall on my face and publicly humiliate myself. I used to panic and literally drive myself and my family crazy, but now I'm able to stop and remind myself that my fears are largely imaginary."

Learning to take risks is an important objective for which eating-disordered teens strive. The biggest risk is making the commitment to get well, since that involves changing familiar if not comfortable ways of thinking and behaving. Risk-taking is often terrifying, so counselors usually advise taking small steps. "At first, I just *thought* about how I might feel if I didn't purge," Liz says. "It was quite a while before I actually restricted my purging, and then I only controlled myself once a day. That was the hardest thing in the world. I was so sure I would fail, and some days I did."

Asking for Help—Avoiding Isolation
As they work for recovery, eating-disordered teens must overcome the tendency to isolate themselves, just as they must learn to reach out to family and friends for advice and support.

Admitting that they are imperfect and that they must rely on others for help goes against everything that seems right and normal, however, and even those who have made progress battle the tendency to be self-sufficient. "I know I need to ask for help, but I don't like to," Hannah says. "If someone offers, I tend to say 'no' at first. I'm convinced they're asking out of pity. Relying on others is very hard for me."

Removing *Should* and *Can't*
Since eating-disordered teens are convinced they don't deserve happiness, they regularly fill their lives with activities they believe they *should* do rather than those they enjoy. For instance, Marcella, a binge eater, felt she should help others rather than take a lunch break. Hannah told herself that she couldn't go out and have fun because she needed to study. Ironically, while most teens are being urged to work hard, discipline themselves, and aim for long-term goals rather than immediate gratification, eating-disordered teens need to learn to be gentler with themselves, to incorporate rewards into their work, and

to enjoy the present while preparing for the future in a way that is not rigid or demanding.

Not Expecting Perfection

Although most eating-disordered teens cannot eliminate their perfectionistic tendencies, they must learn to moderate or control their expectations, both for themselves and for others, if they are going to recover. "Coming from a Christian family, I was taught to be good—you know, helpful, humble, unselfish, loving—to me it all boiled down to being as perfect as possible," Kathy explains. "I expected it from other people, too, and when they weren't perfect, I got upset. I still hate to work with people who goof off and don't take things seriously."

Avoiding Mind Reading

Convinced that the world is a negative, critical place, eating-disordered teens find it difficult not to "mind-read"—that is, assume that they know what everyone is thinking. "If a boy looked at me at the mall, I was sure he was laughing at me," Lori explains. "If a friend didn't answer when I spoke to her—you know, didn't hear me— I was sure she was mad. Now, after counseling, I can catch myself in the middle of mind reading and do a reality check. It's not easy to change my perspective, but I'm going to keep trying."

Basing Success on Internal Strengths

Eating-disordered teens must refocus their attention from external to internal qualities as they work toward recovery. In a world where it is easy to focus on appearance and where beauty and glamour often override qualities such as kindness, unselfishness, and loyalty, making such a change can be difficult. With their poor self-esteem and critical point of view, disordered teens have to work extra hard to accept and appreciate the good qualities they possess. Viewing personal success in terms of character rather than low body weight is difficult for other reasons, too. As Ray points out, "It's hard to rely on—and build success on—inner strengths when you're convinced you don't have any."

Establishing an Identity Apart From an Eating Disorder

Establishing an identity apart from an eating disorder is important, since teens must find something besides food on which to focus if they are to recover. For teens who are depressed, afraid to take risks, want to be perfect at everything they try, and believe they are worthless and untalented, getting involved in new activities is just one more chore they must push themselves to do.

New activities often reveal surprising talents, however, and give them the confidence to continue to expand their outlook. "At my counselor's suggestion, I got a job for the first time," Michael says. "It got me out of the house, helped me meet new people, and restored the nerve I lost when I dropped out of school. For the first time, I felt like a grown-up."

Establishing a new identity takes time and commitment, but the process is necessary if a teen is to become a healthy, functioning adult.

Even after eating-disordered teens are well into recovery, they face obstacles and challenges that can sidetrack success. Some get discouraged and drop out of therapy before they complete treatment. Some discontinue treatment with one therapist, find a new one, and start afresh. Some who see themselves as completely recovered encounter new crises and have to return to therapy for further guidance and support.

All face other hurdles as well—coping with personal misconceptions, physical changes, cultural pressure, and family expectations. These and other challenges, along with strategies to successfully overcome them, are explored in the following chapter.

Chapter Six

THE CHALLENGE OF RECOVERY

Marcella's Story

Although Marcella was twenty-eight years old and married when she began treatment for compulsive overeating, she had been overweight for years. In fact, she had begun to eat in response to her emotions in junior high, when the pressures to fit in, dress right, and run with the right crowd had become overpowering. Food was a comfort when she felt left out, and her weight gave her an excuse for being unpopular with the boys. "I had plenty of friends, but few dates. I pretended that was all right, you know. Made the best of things. Whenever a dance came along, a few of us girls would have our own celebration and—yes—it usually involved eating."

Marcella came from a family of dieters and conscientiously tried to lose weight by restricting fat and calories. With every diet, however, her will-

power would crumble after a few days or weeks. She never tried to understand that her failure was usually linked to feelings of anger, sadness, or boredom. "My true 'skinny' self was trapped in a whale-size body, and I tried not to think about it," she says. "I welcomed the times when I was busy doing something else, something that took my mind off eating. I certainly wasn't going to take that time to try and figure out why I was such a freak."

Not a person to sit around and mope, Marcella was involved in many high-school activities and got a great deal of satisfaction from helping others through the service organizations she joined. After graduation, she went on to get married and become a nurse. Immersed in her professional duties, she often found herself too busy for meals. "I worked hard all day, and food was my reward. I usually skipped breakfast and lunch, and by dinner I was exhausted and famished. Often I'd opt for drive-through fast food and usually ordered the biggest meal on the menu. I wasn't picky. In fact, I scarcely bothered to taste what I ate—just gobbled it down on the way home."

After nursing her brother through a long, agonizing illness that eventually took his life, Marcella sought counseling for posttraumatic stress syndrome, insomnia, and inability to concentrate. The pain of watching a loved one suffer and die had caused her to gain a great deal of weight as well. She was 5 feet 5 inches (165 centimeters) and 275 pounds (125 kilograms) and knew that her obesity put her at risk for heart attack, diabetes, and stroke.

Marcella discovered that antidepression medication helped her outlook; soon she was sleeping better, and her concentration improved. When the counselor suggested that they work on her weight problem, Marcella readily agreed. She wanted to lose weight but was leery when the counselor recommended that she quit dieting. "After years of counting calories and restricting food I was a blimp. What would I be like if I ate whatever and whenever I wanted? It was almost too scary to contemplate," she says.

Several counseling sessions convinced Marcella that years of dieting hadn't worked, and she agreed to give her counselor's methods a try. She began by buying a watch with an alarm, which she set to go off every two hours. "I would stop whatever I was doing, close my eyes, put my hand over my stomach, and ask myself if I was truly, physically hungry. If I was, I'd eat, but only after I thought about what my body—not my mouth—wanted and needed. For instance, I loved chips, but they always made me thirsty. When I ate fruit for a snack, it quenched my thirst, supplied the vitamins and fiber my body needed, and took longer to eat, too."

As a symbol of her freedom from dieting, Marcella defiantly sledgehammered her scales to pieces early in therapy. This determination never to diet again alarmed her husband, who attended counseling sessions himself to overcome his fear that his wife was going to extremes with her new eating plan.

Eight months later, on a visit to the doctor, Marcella stepped on a scale and discovered that she had lost more than 100 pounds (45 kilograms). Rather than being joyous, she found that the news revived many feelings that she thought she had forgotten. "The word diet popped back into my head again," Marcella remembers. "I'd been eating according to what my body wanted, but now I started thinking, 'If I cut back a little, eliminate some calories here and there, I could lose more weight.'"

WHAT DOES RECOVERY MEAN?

There are no formal criteria that define what recovery from an eating disorder entails, but therapists generally consider clients recovered when they never or seldom turn to dysfunctional food behaviors to deal with their problems. This may mean that an anorexic never again restricts food, or that she keeps her weight at a low but healthy level. A bulimic may give up chaotic eating altogether, or she may at times overeat in response to her emotions before returning to healthy eating on her own. "Clients define how recovered they want to be," explains one counselor. "The more healthy coping mechanisms they develop, the better they're able to manage their lives."

Since the study of eating disorders is relatively recent in origin, statistics on long-term recovery are incomplete and possibly inaccurate. Evidence seems to show that with treatment about 60 percent of eating-disordered individuals recover totally from their illness and go on to lead normal lives. They establish careers, get married, have children, and are able to cope with the stresses and strains of everyday life. Many of these individuals testify that they are stronger and more insightful than they would have been if they had not been through the trauma of an eating disorder.

Despite treatment, about 20 percent of anorexics and bulimics make only partial recoveries. These individuals still focus on food and weight, battle depression, and exhibit poor social skills, but they are able to survive, hold jobs, make a few friends, and function marginally.

At 95 pounds, this teen is 25 pounds healthier than she was at the worst stage of her anorexia. Recovering from an eating disorder can be a slow, painful process, but a healthy life is the reward.

Another 20 percent of eating-disordered individuals fail to make even a partial recovery. They live lives of quiet desperation, trapped by depression, loneliness, and feelings of helplessness and despair. Most repeatedly show up in emergency rooms and hospitals as the long-term effects of their disorders affect their health and shorten their lives. About 2–3 percent of those individuals who receive treatment eventually die of their disorders. That number is much higher, up to 20 percent, for those who do not seek treatment.

THE CHALLENGES

Eating-disordered teens who commit to recovery still encounter challenges throughout their lifetimes that they must face and overcome if they are to maintain health and happiness. Not every challenge can be included here, since each person's life story is different. Those that are common to most eating-disordered teens, however, include:

- strengthening self-esteem;
- maintaining healthy eating habits;
- accepting physical change;
- coping with criticism and rejection;
- dealing with social pressures;
- handling family expectations;
- coping with friends and family who eat dysfunctionally;
- managing relapses in recovery.

STRATEGIES FOR SUCCESS

Strategies for Strengthening Self-Esteem

Teens who work toward the goals for recovery discussed in the previous chapter find that their self-esteem almost automatically improves. Other strategies, such as the following, are also useful for modifying self-destructive thinking.

- *Challenge old assumptions.* Teens who habitually have negative feelings about themselves and the world must learn to constantly challenge their old assumptions and replace them with more realistic beliefs. For instance, when tempted to link success with beauty, they might think of people, especially women, whose success is based on intelligence, creativity, and individuality rather than looks.

- *Focus on the "big picture."* Recovering teens can gain confidence and perspective by jotting down in a journal significant events—good and bad, successes and failures—that they experience. Then, in reviewing their entries periodically, they can see for themselves that their achievements were real, that their reverses were not "the end of the world," that bad times pass and good times come again. Reviewing a journal can also help them understand that life is a process and that they have plenty of time to correct mistakes and improve their skills.

- *Be less goal-oriented.* Eating-disordered teens are usually serious, hardworking individuals who live in fear of failure. Doing something "just for the fun of it" can be good for self-esteem, since having a good time takes the place of excelling or trying to be perfect. "I'm learning to value the process rather than having to come away with a perfect product," says Liz, who now enjoys ceramics and keeps a few colorful "failures" in her room as reminders of her purpose.

Strategies for Maintaining Healthy Eating Habits
- *Eliminate distractions.* In working to relate healthfully to food, teens learn to eliminate distractions and concentrate on their food when they eat. This means turning off the television or putting down the book or magazine so that they can notice the smell, taste, and texture of their food.

- *Think about likes and dislikes.* Not everyone likes every food. When teens pay attention to what they eat, they can decide if they enjoy it as much as they thought. "When I started really tasting my food, I discovered that I didn't much like the fatty stuff," Marcella says. "The big surprise was that I didn't like Big Macs. I'd eaten them all my life."

- *Eat to satisfaction.* Recovering teens learn to eat meals and snacks slowly, while thinking about how their stomachs feel as they eat. Anorexics in particular usually find it unpleasant to feel food in their stomachs and may have to make a mental effort to persevere with normal eating until they feel comfortable again.

    All recovering teens must remember to stop eating when they begin to feel satisfied and are no longer hungry. This is difficult for anorexics, whose appetites often become insatiable for a time after they return to normal eating. "I thought my body had gone out of control," says Kathy. "I especially craved stuff I'd denied myself before. My counselor encouraged me to just keep eating until I felt satisfied, and after a while, my appetite got back to normal."

    At the end of a meal recovering teens again pay attention to how they feel—if the food they eat agrees with them, if the eating routine they follow suits their needs.

    "I'm much more comfortable eating several light meals a day rather than a heavy one at night," Marcella explains. "I'm more energetic and I never have to buy antacids anymore."

- *Identify a set point.* Recovering teens are encouraged to allow their bodies to stabilize at a "set point"—the weight they will maintain naturally if they eat when physically hungry and stop when physically satisfied. A set point is sometimes higher than many women prefer. While stabilizing at their set point, binge eaters usually lose weight, while anorexics (and even some bulimics) gain. Maintaining one's weight at its set point, however, is healthy and eliminates the strain and guilt associated with dieting. "I used to weigh every morning, and it set the tone of my day," Marcella says. "Emotionally, I think I was packing those damned scales on my back all the time. I felt ten pounds lighter the day that I threw them away."

Strategies for Coping with Physical Changes

- *Keep in touch with reality.* For binge eaters, losing weight while giving up the stress of dieting is often a positive experience, but anorexics and bulimics find it more difficult to deal with bodies that are larger and curvier (in the case of women) than before. To help combat such feelings, recovering teens learn to look for and remember the things they like about themselves. They practice activities such as listing the things they admire about friends or family, then remembering that these people are likable and worthwhile without having perfect bodies.

    They also remind themselves that even "perfect" models and movie stars do not look the same in real life as they do in magazines and that such pictures are often retouched to remove real-life lumps or blemishes. "When I heard that they air-brushed half an inch off Cindy Crawford's thighs, I felt better," says Lori. "If a top fashion model isn't perfect, none of us can be."

- *Schedule regular medical checkups.* Recovering teens must deal with physical problems that arise from the malnourishment and abuse to which they have subjected their bodies. In most cases, scraggly hair, dry skin, sore throats, and bloated stomachs are temporary annoyances, but some problems can be more serious, even irreversible. Damaged teeth, weakened hearts, fragile bones, infertility, and kidney problems are real threats to long-term health. To identify such problems, to deal with them as soon as they occur, or to prevent complications, doctors recommend regular medical and dental checkups for teens who have been involved in any kind of eating disorder.

Strategies for Coping with Criticism and Rejection

- *Fend off criticism.* To cope with the criticism that can be an everyday part of life, recovering teens learn to question the accuracy of comments and situations that make them feel bad and to give themselves pep talks when they meet with discouragement or rejection. "Before, if someone criticized my work, I was devastated," Marcella says. "Now I feel bad, but I'm able to stop and say 'Wait a minute; they're not perfect either.' Or I look at what I've done and decide it's not that bad."

- *Have a strong support system.* Teens who choose to reveal that they have experienced an eating disorder may face discrimination from those who see them as unstable or mentally ill. Those whose bodies stabilize at a size that is larger than society dictates often face size prejudice in the form of teasing, harassment, and exclusion from jobs, sports, and activities. When this happens, friends and family who are understanding and supportive are invaluable. Being part of a self-help group whose members are sympathetic can also be beneficial. "Not everyone is as kind as I am," Marcella points out. "I used to feel conceited saying something like that, but now I know that kindness is one of my good qualities. One of my gifts."

Strategies for Dealing with Social Pressures

- *Identify misinformation.* In counseling, recovering teens learn to quickly recognize harmful messages on television and in magazines that urge them to overeat and yet remain impossibly thin. Mentally fending off misinformation and replacing it with supportive messages is difficult but possible, especially if teens can see the contradictions in such messages. "Is it fair to lead us to think that we can scarf down bags of potato chips, eat ice cream out of the container, and slather muffins with butter or cream cheese like we see on TV all the time and still remain bone thin?" Liz asks. "I don't think so."

- *Recognize unique needs.* When disordered teens are bombarded with messages that urge them to cut fat, restrict calories, buy exercise equipment, or experiment with diet aids and gimmicks, they remind themselves that such messages are not meant for them, that they know how to maintain their own good health, and that they are likely to fall back into harmful eating and thinking patterns if they give in

116

to such persuasion. "It's interesting to note that there are tons of ads for diet centers on TV just after the holidays and during the summer when we all want to look good in swimming suits," Liz says. "I know it sounds cynical, but I see it as marketing and money. I don't think they really care if we're happy or not."

Strategies for Coping with Family Expectations

- *Get parents involved.* Family support is vital to recovering teens, since parents who understand the process of recovery are more supportive and less likely to undermine a teen's efforts to change. Informed parents can also provide support and encouragement during family reunions or at times when the pressure is on to overeat.

- *Stand firm.* Some family members may never accept the notion that recovering teens are going to be more confident, assertive, and independent. They may be offended when a young person refuses second helpings or leaves food on her plate. In such cases, teens must be prepared to stand firm, despite pressure. "My grandma always wants me to take second helpings, and sometimes she gets a little pushy when I don't," Hannah says. "It used to bother me, but now I just say 'No thanks,' very firmly. I know I don't eat enough yet, but it's my life and my body."

Strategies for Coping with Friends and Family Who Eat Dysfunctionally

- *Recognize danger.* Friends and family who diet, binge on junk food, or practice other unusual or irregular forms of eating are everywhere and represent real danger to recovering teens. That some teens can skirt the edges of an eating disorder without actually developing the full-blown illness tempts many disordered teens to ignore the truth about themselves. "I still think 'so and so' can diet and remain healthy; why can't I?" Liz says. In fact, teens who have suffered from eating disorders are, like alcoholics, at high risk of regressing if they resume dieting, bingeing, or eating emotionally.

- *Resist misguided advice.* Teens must remember that friends and family are products of a food-oriented culture obsessed with thinness. Their intentions are good, but the information and advice they share may jeopardize a successful recovery. Teens need to remind themselves of the misery and discomfort that come with an eating disorder. They must also work to become self-reliant individuals who know what is best for themselves and can resist well-meaning but misguided attempts to help.

Strategies for Coping with Crises and Relapses

- *Accept crises as part of life.* Relapses are a normal part of recovery, since making changes in one's outlook and lifestyle is extremely difficult. Often, relapses occur as a result of some life stress, which might be as minor as a brief illness or as major as a death in the family. Teens who have been deeply entrenched in their disorder—perhaps hospitalized because of it—are more likely to suffer relapses in the course of recovery. Some relapses may be as short as a few days, while others may develop into long-term behaviors that will once again require a period of treatment.

- *Evaluate feelings.* When faced with an over-powering urge to restrict calories, binge, or purge, recovering teens learn to stop and evaluate their feelings, since the urge to eat dysfunctionally is usually a response to something else that is going on in their lives.

- *Turn to new coping mechanisms.* Once such feelings and stresses are identified, teens can turn to one of the new coping mechanisms they have developed. Perhaps they need to work out a solution to the problem. Perhaps they simply need to "sit" with their feelings, knowing that emotions ebb and flow and that they may soon feel better or stronger.

- *Ask for help.* Sometimes, teens may choose to contact a counselor for short-term supportive therapy. During these sessions the therapist listens, reassures, offers advice, and encourages the patient to take responsibility for her life and for maintaining newly developed behaviors.

As discussed in this chapter, not every teen recovers completely from an eating disorder despite the best of intentions and the finest professional care. In the next chapter, you will read about progress being made by the seven young people in this book. Whether they have overcome their disorders or are still working to rebuild their lives, their stories are examples of what can be accomplished when doubt, confusion, and despair are replaced with courage, determination, and hope for the future.

Chapter Seven
SUCCESS STORIES

Teens like those in this book have, to a greater or lesser extent, put aside harmful behaviors that at first seemed vital to their lives. They have confronted unexplored emotions, faced feelings that were shameful or disturbing, and accepted truths that they tried hard to avoid for a long time.

For them, and others like them, there was no set of instructions or how-to books that guaranteed success. They have no assurance that they will not lapse into dysfunctional eating sometime in the future. In fact, they have only their experience, their budding self-esteem, and their newfound coping mechanisms to help them meet the challenges of the future. "I try to take it a day at a time," says Hannah. "For now, I'm dealing with my problems better than before, and I like myself some of the time. That may not be the perfection I once hoped for, but it's better than nothing. It's better than starving myself to death."

LORI'S STORY—
A HEALTHY OUTLOOK

Lori's fear of serious complications was all the motivation she needed to begin curbing her binge-purge behavior. As the numbing effects of the abuse wore off, Lori became aware of the anger and unhappiness she felt. She remained in therapy for two years, concentrating on accepting her body and her size. She was moderately successful at the task, although a doctor's comment that she was overweight and needed to diet set back her progress for several months. She eventually came to terms with her size but still feels large and awkward around smaller people, particularly her parents.

When members of Lori's extended family became aware of her disorder, they treated her as "the bulimic one," asking about her progress, making special concessions when it came to her food and eating, "watching me when they thought I wouldn't notice," Lori remembers. One aunt had the insight to behave in a more relaxed manner, and Lori found this particularly helpful, since it made her feel normal. "I'll always be grateful to my aunt," Lori says. "I don't know how she understood, but she was there when I needed her."

At about the same time, Lori began exploring the spiritual side of her nature, going to church and developing a faith in God. "It was a help to know that I wasn't all alone trying to make these difficult changes in my life," she explains. "Not only did I have my counselor, I had a higher power to support me when I felt like quitting. It made a lot of difference."

At the end of two years, Lori had completely recovered from her eating disorder. She left therapy and has been able to maintain a healthy outlook. "When I look back at the old Lori, I feel sorry for her," she says. "She was so young and unhappy. I'm glad I left her behind. Life isn't perfect now, but it's much better."

RAY'S STORY—
"DECIDING WHAT I WANT TO DO"

As Ray developed coping mechanisms in therapy, he was able to work through the embarrassment he felt about having been teased in elementary school. He revealed to his counselor that some classmates had called him gay, and he admitted that even he sometimes questioned his sexuality.

With his counselor's help, he worked through those concerns. At the same time, he came up with some activities—restoring an old car and going to baseball games—that took the place of his weight-lifting regimen. As he worked these activities into his daily routine, he became more relaxed and happy and was able to reduce his unhealthy eating. "Learning to listen to my body was hard for me," he says. "I'd never thought about what kinds of foods made me feel good physically and which ones didn't. I didn't even understand what the counselor was talking about at first."

During therapy, Ray began examining feelings of anger that he had never acknowledged before. His parents attended some of his sessions, and during discussions, Ray admitted that he had always assumed that they expected him to accomplish great things in his life. "My folks were well-educated, accomplished people. I assumed they would look down on me if I wasn't the same."

Ray came to understand that he needed to focus on what he wanted in life, and he began making progress in dealing with his overeating. He learned to identify when he was angry and what had angered him at any particular time. With great difficulty, he learned to ask for help when he needed it.

Ray is making excellent progress in therapy and has been able to maintain his weight at 200 pounds (91 kilograms). He is enrolled in school, has a girlfriend for the first time, and is developing a spiritual life that gives him a sense of peace and support. He is not comfortable leav-

The incorporation of new skills and activities into a teen's life can make a difference in recovery from an eating disorder. The self esteem this helps to build, along with the understanding that comes from addressing the underlying issues that triggered the disorder, combine to help a young person recover and to stay healthy.

ing therapy yet, however, and schedules once-a-month appointments with his counselor. In therapy he works on his social skills, on impulse control, and on trying to decide what he wants out of life. He understands now that his willingness to believe that his parents controlled his life was a kind of passive power struggle. "When I believed that, I could blame them and be angry, and I didn't have to decide what I wanted to do," he says.

HANNAH'S STORY—
DEVELOPING A NEW ATTITUDE

After five years of treatment, Hannah still struggles with anorexia, depression, and anxiety. She continues to take antidepressants, attends regular counseling sessions, and maintains her weight at a low, but relatively safe, level. She recognizes that many issues remain unresolved in her life and keep her from total recovery. "I still have a lot of trouble with assertiveness," she says. "Lots of times I don't communicate my needs until I'm angry. I still think in terms of black and white, and I drive myself crazy sometimes looking for the perfect solution to every problem that comes up."

With the support of her counselor, Hannah chose to go to college directly after graduation from high school. Coping with the pressure of moving away from home, living among strangers, and eating dorm food was difficult, but she did not give up and now sees the time as a hard but valuable learning experience. "I've become much stronger and more independent in the past few years," she says. "I have new friends, and they seem to like me even when I express my opinion and it's different from theirs. They're the kind of girls who like to laugh and have fun, but they work hard, too. They're good role models for me."

Hannah is still nervous about the future, particularly the day she leaves school and friends behind, but she hopes to be strong enough to handle the change. "I want to be able to face new situations without being totally consumed by fear and anxiety. I want to be able to calm myself down, trust God, and reassure myself that everything will turn out okay," she says. "It will help that I'm beginning to see good qualities in myself—ones that I didn't see or simply disregarded before. I've begun to realize that I can be more than a bone-thin, straight-A student."

MICHAEL'S STORY—
RECOVERY IN PROGRESS

Although he entered therapy voluntarily, it took some time before Michael was ready to admit to and tackle the problems of low self-esteem, poor social and communication skills, lack of purpose, and dependence on his mother that had led to his disorder. When he did, the results were positive. "The counselor asked my folks to come to some of the sessions—quite a few, in fact—and, for the first time, we opened up to one another. Mom talked about her fears, and Dad and I got past the yelling and discussed some stuff that was really bugging us. Turns out he blamed himself all this time for my problems. I'd have never guessed that in a million years!"

Together, Michael and his parents worked on establishing a healthier relationship with one another. As Michael's self-awareness and self-esteem grew, his eating patterns improved, and he was able to make a few friends. New relationships and his work in therapy improved his social skills and self-confidence, but he remains hesitant to become totally independent. He has chosen to continue therapy even though his weight is stable and his counselor considers him recovered from his eating disorder. She states: "Michael's future is positive, provided his self-esteem continues to rise, and he continues to see he has characteristics other than an eating disorder that make him unique, interesting, and worthwhile."

"We talk about me going back to college sometime soon," Michael says. "But I'm not quite ready for that yet. College was a bad time. I want to be sure I'm ready for the challenge when I decide to go."

KATHY'S STORY—
END OF THE POWER STRUGGLE

Because of her depression and the history of depression in her family, Kathy was considered a good candidate for antidepressant medication. With it, her attitude improved, her motivation and concentration increased, and she seemed willing to work on her problems, particularly the power struggle between her and her parents. "It wasn't hard for me to accept that there was something going on between Mom, Dad, and me," she says. "I mean, they were treating me like a two-year-old, for Pete's sake. No one else's parents were forcing them to clean their plate and taking them to the bathroom. It was absolutely ridiculous!"

Kathy and her parents went through eighteen months of family counseling, where they discussed their expectations, the confusion caused by unspoken messages, and their relationships with one another. Although Kathy's parents were hesitant to change, they finally recognized that their daughter's needs were different from their own and began working to give her more independence and to accept her for who she was rather than what she achieved. "It was hard to get it through my head that telling Kathy 'Work hard and do your best' encouraged her perfectionism and hindered her progress," her father says. "I think I understand now. We saw it as being caring parents. She saw it as pressure."

Kathy's decision to take a year away from college was difficult for her parents to accept, as well. It proved beneficial, however, and after four years in therapy, Kathy has made a complete recovery in terms of her eating disorder. She remains something of a perfectionist but uses healthy coping methods to deal with problems as they come along.

"There are still times in my life when I feel like I need a little extra support," she says. "I scheduled a couple of appointments with my counselor after I discovered my mother had cancer, and then again after I learned about my brother's substance abuse. Those were events that I didn't feel I could deal with on my own. I don't think it hurts to have backup support for those times you feel really bad. For some people, it's parents or a friend—for me, it's my therapist. I don't think it matters, as long as you have someone."

LIZ'S STORY— FINDING HER OWN WAY

Despite the crisis that she had undergone, Liz was not eager to begin putting her life back together after her heart attack. She awoke in the hospital extremely depressed, wanting to die, and unhappy that she had been resuscitated. Her only relief was that her parents were arguing over their need for marital counseling. For part of the time at least, their attention was diverted from her. "I don't remember that time very clearly. All I know is that someone told me I was a lucky girl—I disputed that fact wholeheartedly—and that they had set up an appointment with my counselor for as soon as I left the hospital. All I could think was 'Here we go again.'"

Fortunately, Liz's heart attack had caused no cardiac or brain damage. At her parents' insistence she reluctantly went back into treatment, but she was still angry and frustrated and continued to restrict calories and stay at a low weight. Her counselor persisted in working with her, however, urging her to explore her feelings, to express her opinions even if they differed from those of her parents, and to begin to live her life the way she wanted to rather than conform to family expectations. "It was hard for Liz's parents to tolerate who she was and how angry she was," Liz's counselor says. "They were quiet; she was emotional. They saw themselves as middle-of-the-road; she was really a very opinionated young woman."

As Liz began to learn healthier coping skills, her eating disorder abated, although she remained thin. She finished high school but didn't go away to college immediately as her parents had hoped, preferring instead to work and continue counseling at home. Eventually, she did attend college, but again she rejected her parents' advice to become an accountant and went into veterinary medicine. "We didn't think she could handle the stresses of vet school," her mother says. "Accounting seemed so safe and practical. But Liz sees things differently than we do. She made it through and is doing very well. We're delighted that she finally found her own way in life."

MARCELLA'S STORY— "LIFE IS STILL PAINFUL"

With her counselor's help, Marcella successfully resisted the temptation to fall back into dysfunctional eating after she weighed herself in the doctor's office. She continued to monitor her hunger and found that taking time to eat several times a day not only eliminated her uncontrollable urge to devour anything and everything at dinner, but also dissipated the exhaustion she felt at the end of the day. "When I dieted and lost weight before, I felt so tired. It was all I could do to drag myself through the day, and I was grouchy as a bear. This approach is different. I feel better than I ever did before."

Part of Marcella's new lifestyle involved finding ways to work exercise into her routine. Since even mild exercise was an effort, she took a low-key approach at first—

vacuuming, climbing stairs, parking on the outskirts of the parking lot when she went to the mall. With newfound energy, she started walking and then took up jogging, an activity she had enjoyed when she was young. In counseling, she also took time to explore the poor self-esteem, anger, and frustration that she had always tamped down with food.

Marcella remains in therapy, working through other issues that have arisen in her life, particularly the fact that she and her husband appear unable to have children. She observes: "I had to learn that life is painful sometimes, and pain does not automatically go away just because you're doing the appropriate coping skill."

Learning to be oneself, to trust oneself, and to stand up for one's convictions are difficult for any teen, but especially challenging for a disordered teen who continually battles self-doubts and shaky self-esteem. With the support of family and friends, and with the help of dedicated counselors, many teens are learning to become their own best friends, to encourage themselves when they feel discouraged, and to be gentle with themselves when they fail. With time and practice, they are beginning to understand that to be human is to be imperfect and that a person usually has an entire lifetime to learn from mistakes, to right wrongs, and to accomplish goals. Some even feel confident enough to share their hard-won insights with others.

"My advice to kids with eating disorders," says Liz, "is look beyond the surface. That applies to yourself, to your friends, to the stuff you see on TV. And then, don't be afraid to ask for help. There are people out there who know how to help, but you've got to let them. You've got to open up. If you can accept help, and are willing to look at the world from the inside out, you'll have a good chance of getting beyond this thing. You'll have a good chance of reclaiming your life."

GLOSSARY

alkalosis: abnormally high alkalinity of body fluids and blood, which normally are slightly acidic. The condition may cause fatigue, muscle weakness, and other metabolic changes.

ambivalence: the existence of opposing feelings toward a person, object, or idea.

amenorrhea: the cessation or absence of menstruation for more than three months.

anorexia nervosa: an eating disorder that involves the practice of self-starvation.

antidepressants: medications that correct brain chemical imbalances and fight clinical depression.

anxiety: intense dread or fear resulting from the anticipation of a threatening, perhaps unspecified, event.

behavioral therapy: psychological therapy based on modifying a client's behavior, usually through the use of techniques such as anxiety-management training or assertiveness training.

binge: to eat huge amounts of food in a short period of time.

black-and-white thinking: thinking that follows an all-or-nothing pattern and allows for no moderation or compromise. A black-and-white thinker believes statements such as "I am perfect or I am a failure" or "I starve or I binge."

body-image distortion: inaccurate perception of one's own looks in contrast with how one actually looks. For instance, an anorexic hates her body for being fat even though she may be very thin.

bulimia nervosa: an eating disorder that involves consuming large amounts of food and then eliminating that food by vomiting, exercising, or using laxatives and diuretics.

cognitive therapy: psychological therapy intended to change a client's harmful ways of thinking; a technique for helping people think differently so they will act differently.

compulsion: an irresistible impulse to act.

depression: an emotional state characterized by feelings of sadness, lack of energy, and loss of ambition.

diuretics: drugs that act on the kidneys to increase the flow of urine.

dysfunctional: abnormal or impaired in function.

electrolytes: substances that, when dissolved in water, separate into electrically charged particles capable of conducting an electrical current.

esophageal tear: a rupture of the esophagus—the muscular food tube leading from the mouth to the stomach—brought on by the stress of self-induced vomiting.

interpersonal therapy: psychological therapy that aims to help clients improve social skills, resolve problems with family, learn to control anger, etc.

lanugo: fine, downy hair that covers the body of a human fetus and is commonly found on the bodies of anorexics.

neurotransmitters: chemical substances that transmit nerve impulses in the brain.

nutritional therapy: therapy that aims to improve unhealthy eating habits and educate clients about the body's nutritional needs.

obese: significantly overweight, usually more than 20–30 percent above recommended body weight.

obsession: a preoccupation with a fixed idea or unwanted emotion; a persistent, often unreasonable, idea or emotion.

perfectionism: a tendency to be displeased with anything not perfect or not meeting very high standards.

post-traumatic stress syndrome: a mental illness that can develop after a person experiences or witnesses traumatic or life-threatening events. Symptoms can include flashbacks, feelings of guilt, irritability, trouble with concentration, depression, and sleep difficulties that may include nightmares.

purging: eliminating food by vomiting or the use of laxatives, diuretics, or overexercising.

relapse: to regress after partial recovery from an illness; to fall or slide back into a former state.

self-esteem: self-confidence; self-respect.

set point: the genetically programmed weight that is ideal for each individual and that a normally functioning body tries to maintain. Theoretically, if a person eats when hungry and stops when full, his or her weight will naturally stabilize at the set point.

size prejudice: an adverse judgment or opinion, formed without knowledge of the facts, against people who are overweight or heavier than society finds normal and acceptable.

steroids: any of a large group of fat-soluble chemicals. Anabolic steroids, derived from the male hormone testosterone, are used by athletes to increase muscle mass and induce weight gain. Steroids can have serious side effects, including increased aggressive behavior, an increased risk of liver cancer, and heart attack.

RESOURCES

An extensive list of national and international organizations that provide information and help with eating disorders can be accessed over the Internet under Eating Disorders or at the following addresses:

http://www.something-fishy.com
http://www.anred.com

Or you can write to:

American Anorexia/Bulimia Association, Inc. (AABA)
165 West 46th Street, #1108
New York, NY 10036
(212) 575-6200

AABA is a nonprofit organization that publishes a newsletter several times a year. Contact the New York office to find a local chapter in your area. Membership is open to all.

Center for the Study of Anorexia and Bulimia
1 West 91st Street
New York, NY 10024
(212) 595-3449

The center's objectives include effective treatment, specialized training, significant research, and increased community understanding.

Christy Henrich Foundation
PO Box 414287
Kansas City, MO 64141-4287
(816) 395-2611

The foundation is a nonprofit organization dedicated to fighting eating disorders. It was founded in memory of Christy Henrich, an outstanding gymnast who lost her fight with anorexia in 1994.

Eating Disorders Awareness and Prevention, Inc. (EDAP)
603 Stewart Street, Suite 803
Seattle, WA 98101
(206) 382-3587

EDAP provides free and low-cost educational information on eating disorders and their prevention. It sponsors National Eating Disorders Awareness Week nationwide and has a network of educational coordinators who put on programs in schools and communities.

National Eating Disorders Organization (NEDO)
6655 South Yale Avenue
Tulsa, OK 74136
(918) 481-4044

NEDO focuses on treatment referrals, information distribution, prevention, education, and research.

National Association of Anorexia Nervosa and Associated Disorders (ANAD)
Box 7
Highland Park, IL 60035
(847) 831-3438

ANAD sponsors a wide variety of programs, including consumer advocacy, counseling, education, referral lists, and research.

Overeaters Anonymous (OA)
PO Box 44020
Rio Rancho, NM 87124-4020
(505) 891-2664

OA is an international self-help group modeled after the twelve-step program of Alcoholics Anonymous. Local chapters offer meetings and telephone support and encourage service and sponsorship. Check your telephone directory for the number of a local chapter.

The Renfrew Center
475 Spring Lane
Philadelphia, PA 19128
(800) 736-3739

Renfrew is a national women's mental-health center with many locations and a nationwide referral network. It specializes in the treatment of eating disorders, trauma, anxiety, depression, substance abuse, and other women's issues.

FURTHER READING

For Preteens and Teens

Bode, Janet. *Food Fight.* New York: Simon & Schuster, 1997.

Epstein, Rachel. *Eating Habits and Disorders.* New York: Chelsea House, 1990.

Kolodny, Nancy J. *When Food's a Foe.* Boston: Little, Brown, 1987.

Malony, Michael, and Rachel Kranz. *Straight Talk About Eating Disorders.* New York: Facts on File, 1991.

Moe, Barbara. *Coping With Eating Disorders.* New York: Rosen Publishing Group, 1991.

Sonder, Ben. *Eating Disorders: When Food Turns Against You.* New York: Franklin Watts, 1993.

For Older Teens and Adults

Abraham, Suzanne, and Derek Llewellyn-Jones. *Eating Disorders: The Facts*. Oxford, England: Oxford University Press, 1997.

Berg, Frances M. *Afraid to Eat*. Hettinger, ND: Healthy Weight Journal, 1997.

Claude-Pierre, Peggy. *The Secret Language of Eating Disorders*. New York: Random House, 1997.

Costin, Carolyn. *Your Dieting Daughter: Is She Dying for Attention?* New York: Brunner/Mazel, Inc., 1997.

Lemberg, Raymond, ed. *Controlling Eating Disorders With Facts, Advice, and Resources*. Phoenix: The Oryx Press, 1992.

Pipher, Mary. *Reviving Ophelia*. New York: Ballantine Books, 1994.

Sacker, Ira M., and Marc A. Zimmer. *Dying to Be Thin*. New York: Time Warner Books, 1987.

Zerbe, Kathryn J. *The Body Betrayed*. Washington, DC: American Psychiatric Press, 1993.

INDEX

Page numbers in *italics* refer to illustrations.

Abraham, Suzanne, 21
achievement-oriented parents, influence of, 71–72
alcohol abuse, 43, 57, 72
Alcoholics Anonymous (AA), 98
alkalosis, 42
amenorrhea, 25, 35, 38
American Psychiatric Association, 25, 34
anorexia nervosa, 20. (*see also* eating disorders)
    behavioral symptoms of, 36–37
    binge-purge type, 37, 43

diagnosis of, 34–35
effects of, 23–24
first use of term, 25
incidence of, 29
mortality rate from, 38
physical symptoms of, 37–38
psychological symptoms of, 40
Anorexia Nervosa and Related Eating Disorders (ANRED), 26
antidepressants, 30, 58, 98–99
anti-obesity drugs, 99–100
anxiety, 20, 26, 42, 58, 98
arthritis, 46
Asian-Americans, 29

beauty ideal, 27, 58–60
behavioral therapy, 90–91
Berg, Frances M., 92
binge-eating disorder, 20, 24–
    26. (*see also* eating
    disorders)
    behavioral symptoms
        of, 43–44, 46
    diagnosis of, 35–36
    incidence of, 29–30
    physical symptoms of,
        46
    psychological symp-
        toms of, 46–47
biological factors in eating
    disorders, 56–58
black-and-white thinking, 53,
    90
blacks, 29
blame, 100–101
bloating, 38, 42
bodybuilding, *19*, 78
body image dissatisfaction,
    27, 28, 35–38, 40, 43–
    44, 51, 58–60
body weight, 34–35, 47, 48
boyfriends, influence of, 77
breast cancer, 46
Bruch, Hilde, 25
bulimia nervosa, 20. (*see also*
    eating disorders)
    behavioral symptoms
        of, 40–41
    diagnosis of, 35
    effects of, 24
    incidence of, 29
    mortality rate from, 42
    physical symptoms of,
        41–42
    psychological symp-
        toms of, 42–43

Bulimics Anonymous (BA),
    97, 98

cardiac arrest, 42
Carpenter, Karen, *14*, 15
Carpenter, Richard, *14*
childbirth, 46
chipmunk cheeks, 42
clothing, 37
cognitive therapy, 90
cold intolerance, 38, 46
compulsions, 57, 58
compulsive overeating (*see*
    binge-eating disorder)
concentration, 38, 56
conflict resolution, 78–81
conservative parents, influ-
    ence of, 71
constipation, 25, 38
counseling, 78, 80
Crawford, Cindy, 115
critical parents, influence of,
    72

dancers, 28, 62
dehydration, 42
depression, 26, 30, 40, 48,
    56, 57
dexphenfluramine (Redux),
    46, 99
diabetes, 46
*Diagnostic and Statistical
    Manual of Mental
    Disorders* (DSM-IV), 34
dieting, 44, 46, 64
diet pills, 28, 41, 44, *45*
diuretics (water pills), 24, 35,
    42
dizziness, 38
dreams, 40
drug abuse, 43, 57, 72

dysfunctional parents, influence of, 72

eating disorders. (*see also* anorexia nervosa, bulimia nervosa)
biological factors, 56–58
case stories, 11–13, 15–18, 20, 32–34, 49–51, 66–68, 82–85, 106–109, 121–122, 124–129
causes of, 26–27
complexity of, 15
diagnostic criteria for, 34–36
effects of, 23–24
family relationships and, 64–65, 68–74, 117–118
gender and, 27–28
history of, 25–26
home environment and, 26, 51, 54–56
incidence of, 27, 29–30
minorities and, 28–29
peer relationships and, 27, 74–75, 76, 77–78
persons at risk for, 27–29
recovery from, 30–31, 106–119
roots of, 51–54
severity of symptoms, 47–48
social pressures and, 27, 51, 58–61, 116–117
treatment of (*see* treatment)

triggers for, 61–62, 63, 64–65
understanding, 20
entertainment industry, 62, 64
esophageal tears, 42
estrogen, 38
exercise, vigorous, 24, 35, 39, 41

fainting spells, 38
family relationships, 64–65, 68–74, 117–118
family therapy, 89, 96, 97
fasting, 24, 28, 35, 41
fat cells, 43
feelings, suppression of, 54
fenfluramine-phentermine (fen-phen), 46, 99
fenfluramine (Pondimin), 99
fluvoxamine (Luvox), 98
Food and Drug Administration (FDA), 99
Food Guide Pyramid, 22

gallbladder disease, 46
gastric bypass, 46
gender, eating disorders and, 27–28
genetics, 26, 51
girlfriends, influence of, 75, 76, 77
goal-setting, realistic, 101
group therapy, 95
growth, stunting, 24
Gull, William, 25
gymnasts, 28, 62, 63

hair loss, 46
heart attack, 46

heartbeat, 38, 42
Henrich, Christy, *63*
high blood pressure, 46
Hispanics, 29
home environment, 26, 51, 54–56
hospitalization, 86–87, *87*, 92–93

individual therapy, 94–95
inferiority, feelings of, 52
insomnia, 56
interpersonal therapy, 91
irritability, 40, *56*
isolation, 40, 102

Janet, Pierre, 25
jaw wiring, 46
junk food, *10*, 23

Kolodny, Nancy J., 15

lanugo hair, 38
laxatives, 24, 28, 35, 41, 42
Llewellyn-Jones, Derek, 21

malnutrition, 38
materialism, 27
medical checkups, 115
medications, 57, 98–100
menstrual cycles, 25, 35, 38
Meridia, 99
mind reading, avoidance of, 103
minorities, eating disorders and, 28–29
models, 58, *59*, 62, 115
Moe, Barbara, 97
mortality rate, 38, 42, 110
Moss, Kate, *59*

needs, unsatisfied, 55–56
negative mind-set, 52–53, 72
neurotransmitters, 57, 98
normal eating, defined, 21–23
nutritional therapy, 92

obesity, 43, 46, 47
obsessions, 57–58, 99
osteoporosis, 38
Overeaters Anonymous (OA), 96, 98
overexercising, 24, 35, *39*, 41
over-the-counter diet pills, 44, *45*

parents (*see* family relationships)
Paxil, 98
peer relationships, 27, 74–75, *76*, 77–78
perfectionism, 53–54, 103
personality traits, 26, 51
pessimism, 40, 53
Phillips, Jeanne, 100
physical abuse, 72, 73
power struggles, 79
Prozac, 30, 98
pulse rate, 25

recovery, 30–31, 106–119
    goals of, 100–105
Redux, 46, 99
relapses, 118–119
risk-taking, 101–102

scare tactics, 79
secrecy, 451
selective serotonin reuptake inhibitors (SSRIs), 98

self-esteem, 20, 27, 46, 52,
    64, 65, 72
    strategies for strengthen-
        ing, 111–112
self-help groups, 96–98,
    116
set point, 114
sexual abuse, 72, 73
siblings, effects of eating
    disorders on, 74
single-parent families, 73
size prejudice, 72, 77, 116
sleep, 38
social pressures, 27, 51, 58–
    61, 116–117
sports, 28, 62, 63, 78
stomach acids, 42
stroke, 46
Stunkard, Albert, 25
suicidal thoughts, 48, 56

teachers, 61–62
tooth enamel, 42
track, 62
treatment, 30–31, 82–100
    accurate diagnosis, 85–
        86
    behavioral therapy,
        90–91
    choosing counselor or
    therapist, 87–88

cognitive therapy, 90
family therapy, 89, 96,
    97
frequency and duration
    of, 94
group therapy, 95
hospitalization, 86–87,
    87, 92–93
individual therapy, 94–
    95
interpersonal therapy, 91
medications, 98–100
nutritional therapy, 92
preliminary assessment,
    89
resistance to, 86
self-help groups, 96–98
settings for, 92–93

unspoken parental messages,
    69–71

vegetarians, 62
vomiting, self-induced, 24,
    25, 28, 35, 41, 42

women, role of, 27, 60–61
worthlessness, feelings of, 52
wrestling, 62

Zoloft, 98